D1059566

TRICKS & GAMES
ON THE
POOL TABLE

By
FRED HERRMANN

DOVER PUBLICATIONS, INC.
NEW YORK

Published in Canada by General Publishing Company, Ltd., 30 Lesmill Road, Don Mills, Toronto, Ontario.

Published in the United Kingdom by Constable and Company, Ltd.

This Dover edition, first published in 1967, is an unabridged and unaltered republication of the work originally published by the "Tricks" Publishing Company in 1902 under the title *Fun on the Pool Table*.

Standard Book Number: 486- 21814-7
Library of Congress Catalog Card Number: 67-17985

Manufactured in the United States of America
Dover Publications, Inc.
180 Varick Street
New York, N. Y. 10014

PREFACE.

Doubtless a good many of our readers have seen tricks performed on the pool and billiard table by professionals and have considered them wonderful, which they most certainly are, and have been acquired only by a great deal of practice and patience; but how many amateurs would think of attempting to perform them? They know that they are beyond their power, so they are content, as a rule, to *speak* about them, and to *tell* their friends what they *saw*, but unfortunately they cannot *show* them how they were done. In this book we propose to show and illustrate with illustrations that there are many simple and amusing games and tricks on the pool table well within the reach of the most moderate pool player, shots that require no great execution or power of cue to perform, and yet are of sufficient difficulty and contain enough elements of fun to interest good and indifferent players alike, with *no risk of cutting the cloth.*

We have collected here some odd tricks and games, some of them old. This book may, however, be of use to you to refresh your memory, but to those to whom they are new it may serve to while away and afford amusement for an evening and help to relieve the tedium of a rainy hour or two.

CONTENTS.

		PAGE
1.	To Hit the Top Ball First,	11
2	To Pocket Three Balls in One Shot,	12
3.	Round the Woodwork,	12
4.	Hand Carom,	14
5.	Weight Reducer,	16
6.	Pyramid Solitaire,	16
7.	The Match that Cannot be Knocked Down,	18
8.	The Travelling Billiard Balls,	19
9.	To Knock a Coin from the Top of a Ball Out of a Small Ring.	20
10.	Pass Ball Trick,	20
11.	To Make a Coin Describe a Curve and Roll into a Pocket,	22
12.	Tricky Carom,	22
13.	Pyramids: One Pocket Against Five,	24
14.	Run a Ball Off Two Cues,	24
15.	How to Knock a Small Coin from under the Cushion,	26
16.	Quarter in the Pocket,	26
17.	Steeplechase Shot,	28
18.	To Pocket a Ball through Match Boxes.	28
19.	Deceptive Pocket Shot,	30
20.	Pass Through Hand Shot,	30
21.	A Pretty Carom,	32
22.	Squeeze Shot,	32
23.	To Pocket Three Balls in Same Middle Pocket in Two Shots,	34
24.	A New Stroke,	34
25.	Trick Hand Carom,	36
26.	The Hatchet Stroke,	36
27.	Straight Aiming,	38
28.	To Pocket Three Balls in One Shot,	38
29.	Pool Deck Quoits,	40
30.	Balk Practice,	40

PAGE
31. To Pocket Three Balls in Top Pocket in One Shot, ... 42
32. Caroms vs. Pyramids, ... 42
33. To Pocket Three Balls in Same Pocket in One Shot, . . . 44
34. Red into Balk Twenty Times, ... 44
35. The War Game, ... 46
36. Wet Cue Trick, ... 46
37. To Pocket Three Balls in Reverse Order Top Pocket, . . 48
38. Tricky Pocket Shot, ... 48
39. To Go into the Middle Pocket Off the Red Without Moving the White Ball Placed on Centre Spot, ... 50
40. To Pocket Three Balls in One Shot, Middle Pockets, . 50
41. Pyramid Balls Along a Cushion, ... 52
42. Carom Through a Hat, ... 52
43. Three Cues on the Table, ... 54
44. Hand Pocketing Competition, ... 56
45. The Running Shot, ... 56
46. To Hit the Last Ball First, ... 58
47. Game with a Plate on the Table, ... 60
48. To Run a Balanced Ball Along Two Cues . . . 60
49. To Pocket Three Balls in Three Pockets in One Shot, . . 62
50. Solitaire, or Table Golf, ... 62
51. Kiss in Off, ... 64
52. To Carom Without Touching a Ball, ... 66
53. The Lung Test, ... 66
54. Carom Two Corks, ... 66
55. To Pocket Three Balls in Reverse Order—Bottom Pocket, . 68
56. Carom Length of the Table, ... 68
57. Carom into a Hat, ... 70
58. Steady Hands Wanted, ... 70
59. Stop Spinning Ball, ... 70
60 Knock Down a Match, ... 72
61 To Pick up a Quarter, ... 72
62. To Balance a Coin, ... 72
63. To Pocket a Wine Glass, ... 74
64. Race Horses, ... 76
65. Interesting Tricks in Elasticity, ... 78
66 To Pocket Three Balls in the Opposite Middle Pocket in Two Shots, ... 80
67. Chance Encounter Carom, ... 82
68 One Ball on Three, ... 82
69. Five Carom, ... 84

PAGE
70. Pick up a Ball with Two Others, ... 84
71. To Pocket Four Balls in Four Shots, ... 86
72. Collision Shot, ... 86
73. To Jump a Coin into a Glass, ... 88
74. Endless Caroms, ... 88
75. To Pocket Three Balls in Three Different Pockets—Three Shots, 90
76. Switchback Carom, ... 92
77. Fine Off Red Ball, ... 94
78. Wet Finger Trick, ... 94
78. The Imperceptible Jump, ... 94

No. 1.

TO HIT THE TOP BALL FIRST.

Place two balls up against the top cushion, both balls touching, and balance another ball on top of them. (The way to balance the top ball is to rub some chalk in the palm of your hand and rub the ball on it, then it will adhere slightly to the other two balls.) Then play with another ball from balk. The trick is to hit the top ball first. For example: aim carefully at the top ball, hit your ball just sufficiently hard to reach the top cushion, and while the ball is travelling either thump hard on the table with the hand, or give the table a good push with the side of the body. This will cause the top ball to lose its balance, and it will roll gently and straight on to the table between the other two balls before your ball has had time to reach it, the other two balls getting out of the way, and your ball if struck accurately will hit it.

No. 2.

TO POCKET THREE BALLS IN ONE SHOT.

Place the red ball on the pyramid spot with a white ball absolutely touching it in a dead straight line with the left-hand corner of the left top pocket, as in illustration. The trick is to play with another ball from balk, and pocket all three balls in one shot. For example: Place the ball you are going to play with about two inches on the inside of the right-hand spot of the D. Aim to go in off the white into the left-hand corner top pocket, the other white should go into the right-hand top corner, and if you have placed the balls accurately and aimed truly, the red ball should follow yours into the pocket. Medium strength.

No. 3.

ROUND THE WOODWORK.

A very amusing game, and one that requires great steadiness of hand, is to take a ball right round the woodwork of a pool table with the side of a cue.

For example: Put a ball on the woodwork of the table, and put your cue on it about eighteen inches from the tip. Push it little by little without touching the ball with the hand; of course the difficulty lies in rounding the narrow rims of the pockets. It helps you to grip the ball if you chalk the sides of the cue.

Two can play this game at once by starting at different ends of the table.

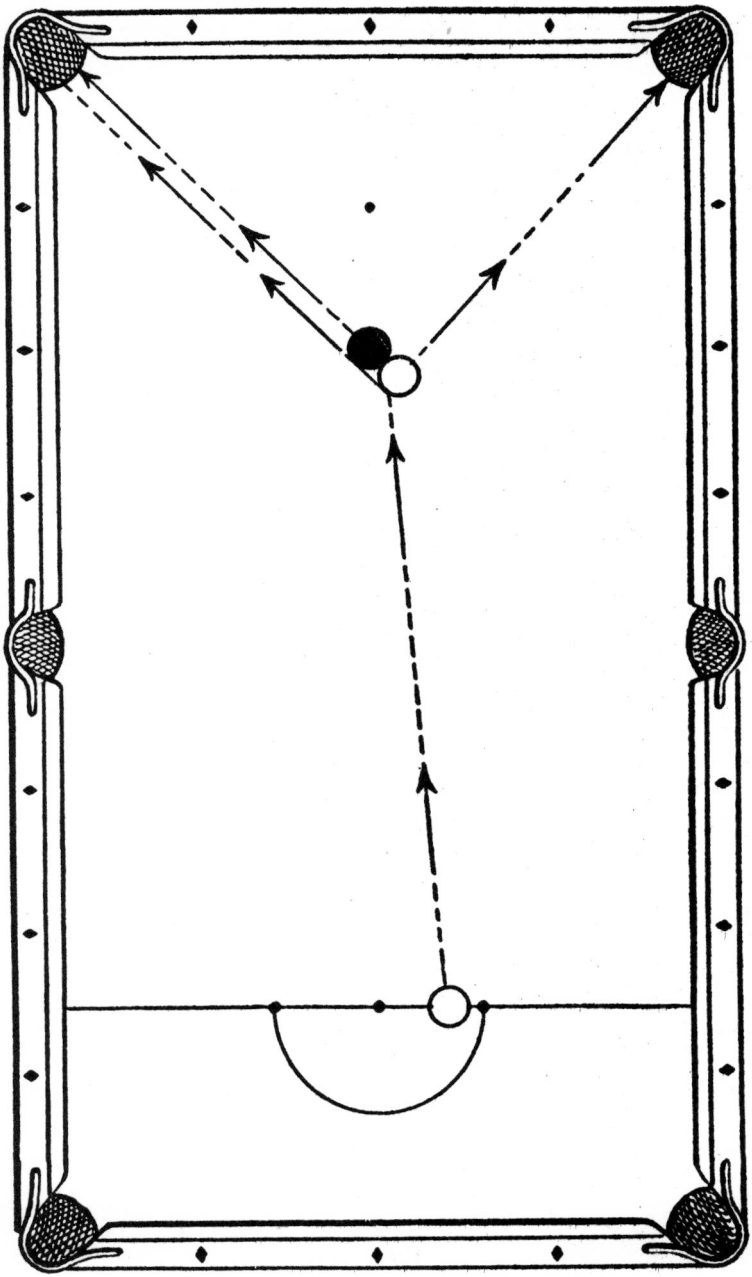

No. 2.

No. 4.

HAND CAROM.

The following carom can be done pretty regularly with a little practice, and though effective is not so difficult as it looks.

Place three balls as in illustration, two balls touching each other on one cushion, the other ball touching cushion exactly opposite, all three being in a straight line; the object is to make a hand carom, playing with a solitary ball. For example: Place the palm of the right hand against the ball with the fingers toward the bottom pocket, and the side of the hand touching the table. Then pull the right arm backward, fairly sharp, toward the top cushion—the ball will work along from the palm to the tips of the fingers—then let go. It should then travel on to the top cushion, and you have unconsciously put on "English," which should throw it across the table as shown in the dotted lines in the illustration. Try it once or twice to get the idea, and the whereabouts to place the balls; as some cushions take side more freely than others, it may be necessary to place the balls farther from or nearer to the bottom cushion.

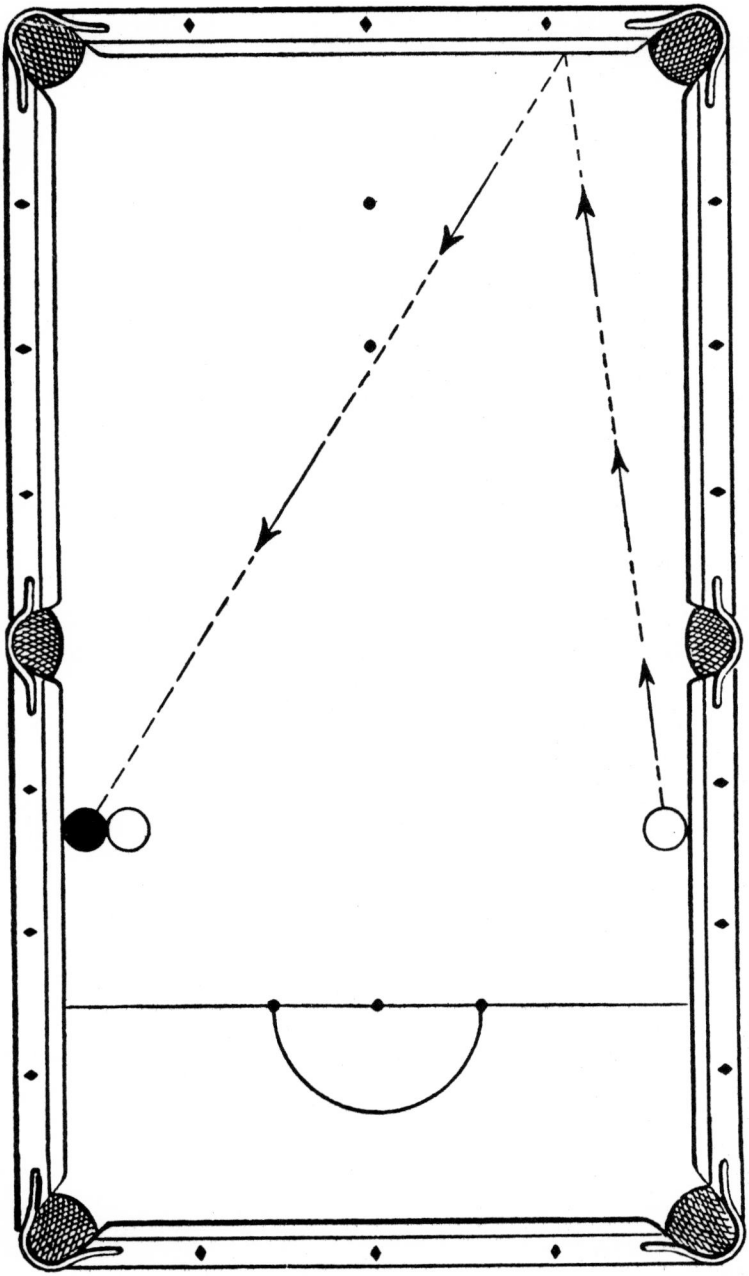

No. 4.

No. 5.

WEIGHT REDUCER.

This is a fine game for getting rapidly into condition, but is best played in the winter. It takes a really active person to accomplish it.

Place a cue on the table, close to the bottom cushion, tip pointing to right-hand bottom pocket. Take a ball in the right hand. The game is to roll a ball up the table, hit the top cushion with sufficient strength that when the ball returns and hits the cue it will jump off the table. See illustration for about the angle. But while the ball is travelling, you have to run round the top of the table and catch it, after it has jumped the table, but before it touches the ground. Stand for the start with the right foot level with the balk line, then roll the ball, and off you go. If you are quick you ought just to be round in time to catch it with your left hand. *Vice versâ* for left-handed players.

No. 6.

PYRAMID SOLITAIRE.

A good game for practice by one's self, and makes an interesting competition.

Place the fifteen pyramid balls on the table in the usual way. The game is to see in how few strokes you can pocket them all, starting from balk in the usual manner. The ordinary rules of pyramid are to apply. If there are many competitors, the number of strokes should be named at which each player must relinquish his attempt. You can handicap good and bad players by giving or taking away strokes.

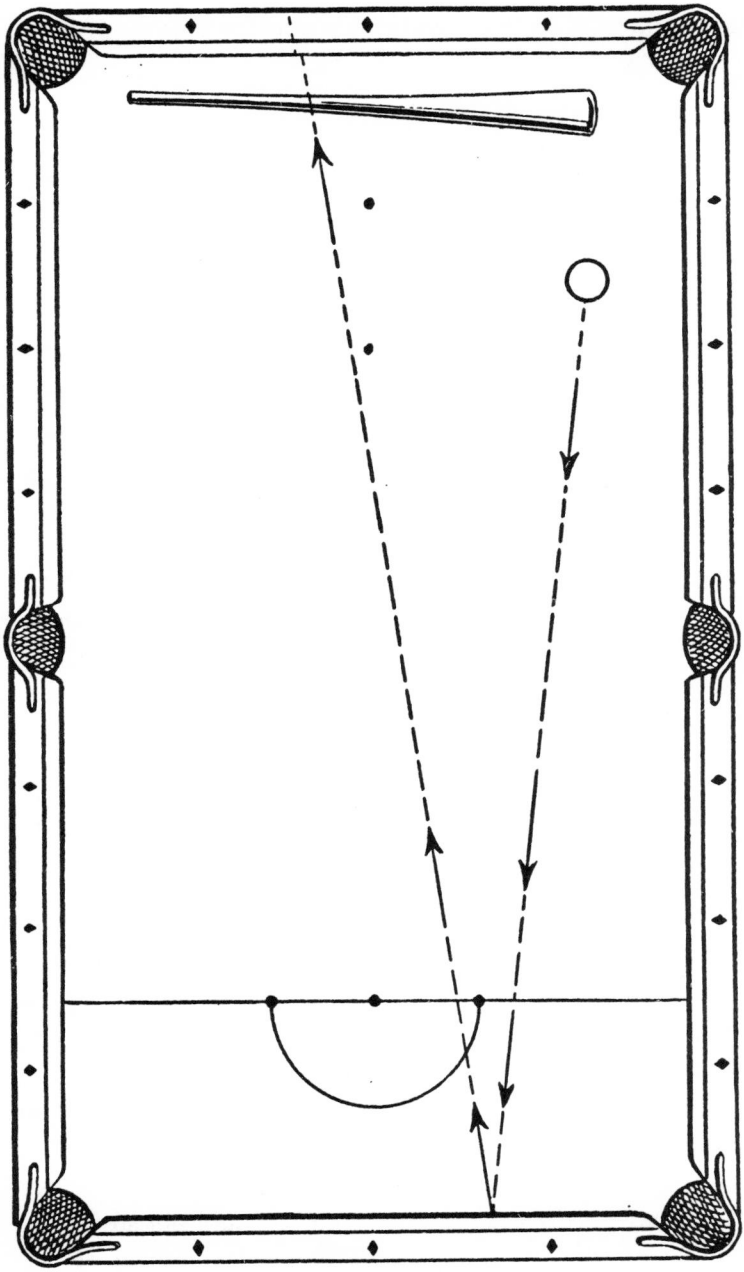

No. 5.

No. 7.

THE MATCH THAT CANNOT BE KNOCKED DOWN.

This is a very curious trick, and will give rise to much amusement, as it is apparently so easy to do. First, stand a match on the table—this may be done by slitting the end a little way up and spreading out, so as to form a small tripod arrangement, or by cutting a slit in a piece of card and placing the end of the match inside the slit; the card will then lie flat on the table. But both these methods must be on a very small scale, as the object is simply to make the match stand upright. Now place three balls round the match, each one touching the other. The match is then standing up in the small space left between the centre of the balls, but is not touched by any one of them. You then invite any one to try and knock the match down by placing their ball about two feet away from the three. They are at liberty to try from any direction outside the two-feet radius.

Strange to say, however hard the balls are struck, the match still remains upright; the reason being that, owing to the position of the balls, they kiss each other away from the centre. The shot, however, may be done by using a little thought. Those who try it for the first time think that they have only to hit the balls hard, and it is sure to go over; but the harder they strike, the firmer the match seems to remain.

One way is to make your ball jump on top of the others; but this is very difficult to judge, and I should not advise any but professionals to attempt it, owing to the danger of cutting the cloth. The other way is to put your ball opposite one of the corners of the triangle and play a run-through shot. Strike your ball well above the centre fairly hard; when it comes in contact with the first ball, it will rebound from the other two, but your ball following on behind will push it forward again, and the match will go over.

No. 8.

THE TRAVELLING BILLIARD BALLS.

This experiment can be accomplished with a fair amount of practice. One cue is laid upon the table and a ball stood upon it; upon this first ball the second one is placed, and then the other cue is rested on top of both balls. In this condition, by picking up both cues, the balls will remain

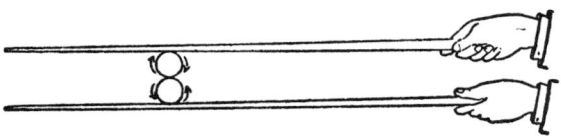

stationary, as in illustration. By gently altering the position of the cues, both balls can be made to run backward and forward without overbalancing. This is because one ball revolves forward and the other revolves in the opposite direction, as is explained by the little arrow upon either side of the balls.

This genuine experiment has been cleverly burlesqued by causing both balls to be attached to the topmost cue. The underneath one is then removed, and the trick, as it were, shown up; this generally occasions a hearty laugh.

No. 9.

TO KNOCK A COIN FROM THE TOP OF A BALL OUT OF A SMALL RING.

Draw a small ring with chalk around the billiard spot three and one-half inches in diameter. Then place a ball on the spot and balance a coin on top of it. The trick is to hit the ball with another ball played from balk, and knock the coin away so that it falls outside the chalk ring. There are two ways of doing this, though neither of them is a certainty every time. The first way and the more difficult is to play with just sufficient strength to reach the object ball and to touch it so slightly that it turns very slowly over and throws off the coin. The other way is to aim so truly that your ball follows straight on after hitting the other ball, catches the coin and knocks it away before it has time to reach the table.

No. 10.

PASS BALL TRICK.

Place a red ball almost in the jaws of a pocket, and a white ball touching the cushion above it about a foot away. The trick is to pocket the white in the nearest pocket, playing with a cue, without touching the red, jumping over it, playing across the table, or a *massé* shot. For example: Take a cue and press the tip against the white, well below the centre, at the angle shown in illustration. This will cause the ball to run up on to the cushion, the cue remaining on top of the ball. Gently rotate the cue to the right, the ball will naturally travel to the left along the cushion past the red, and drop into the pocket.

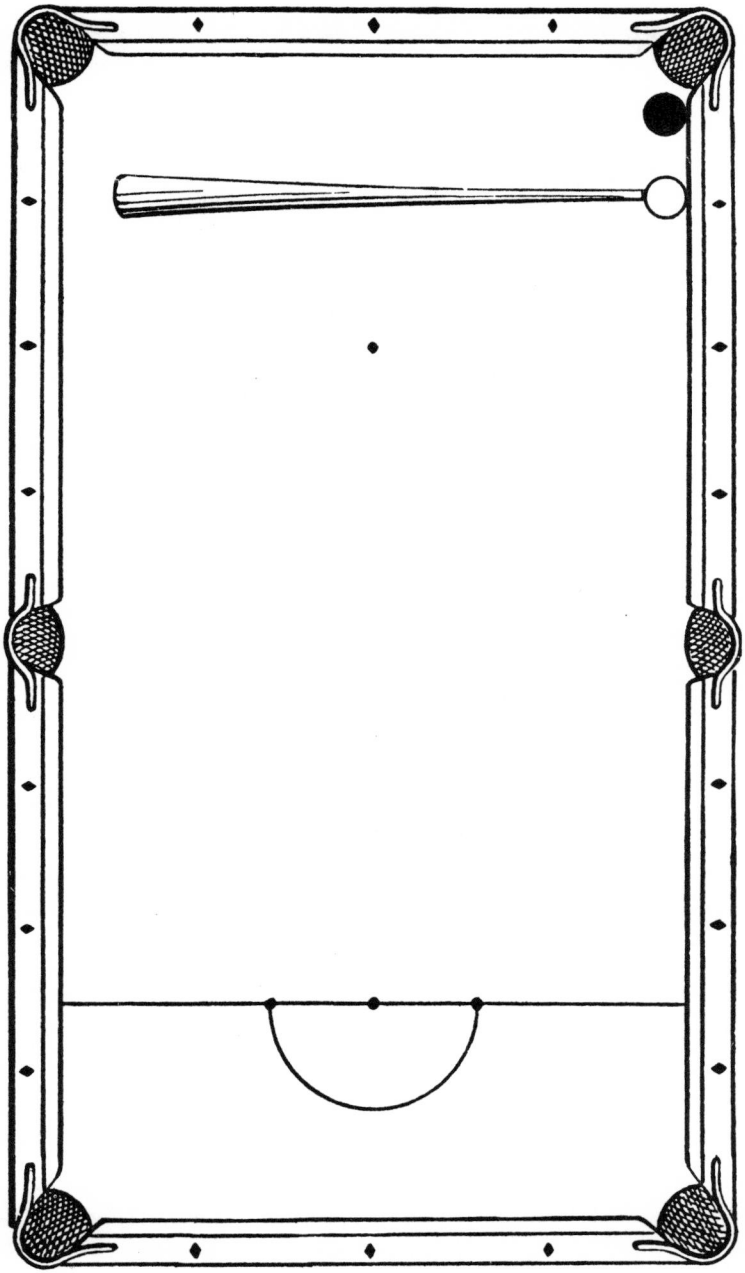

No. 10.

No. 11.

TO MAKE A COIN DESCRIBE A CURVE AND ROLL INTO A POCKET.

A quarter is placed on its edge resting against a cushion about two to three inches above the balk line, left-hand side, and a ball is laid at about the middle of the left-hand top cushion, which it touches. It therefore appears impossible to get the coin in the top left-hand pocket as the ball is apparently in the way, but with a little practice it may be done as follows: The coin, which is to be as nearly upright as possible, must be struck rather high on its edge or it will not roll, and if played properly it will describe a graceful curve right round the ball into the pocket. If the coin is placed leaning slightly and struck gently, it will roll along the cushion and drop into the middle pocket.

No. 12.

TRICKY CAROM.

Place the red ball tight up against the middle of the top cushion with a white ball touching it in a straight line with the billiard spot. Place the other white on the centre spot of the D, therefore the three balls should be in a straight line as in illustration. The shot is to make a carom playing with a ball from balk. It can be done from the side cushions, but it is by no means a certainty that way. To do it pretty regularly you must aim into the jaws of either of the top pockets, hitting the top cushion first. If played fairly hard, the ball will be thrown off by the jaws of the pocket right along the top cushion and your carom is made.

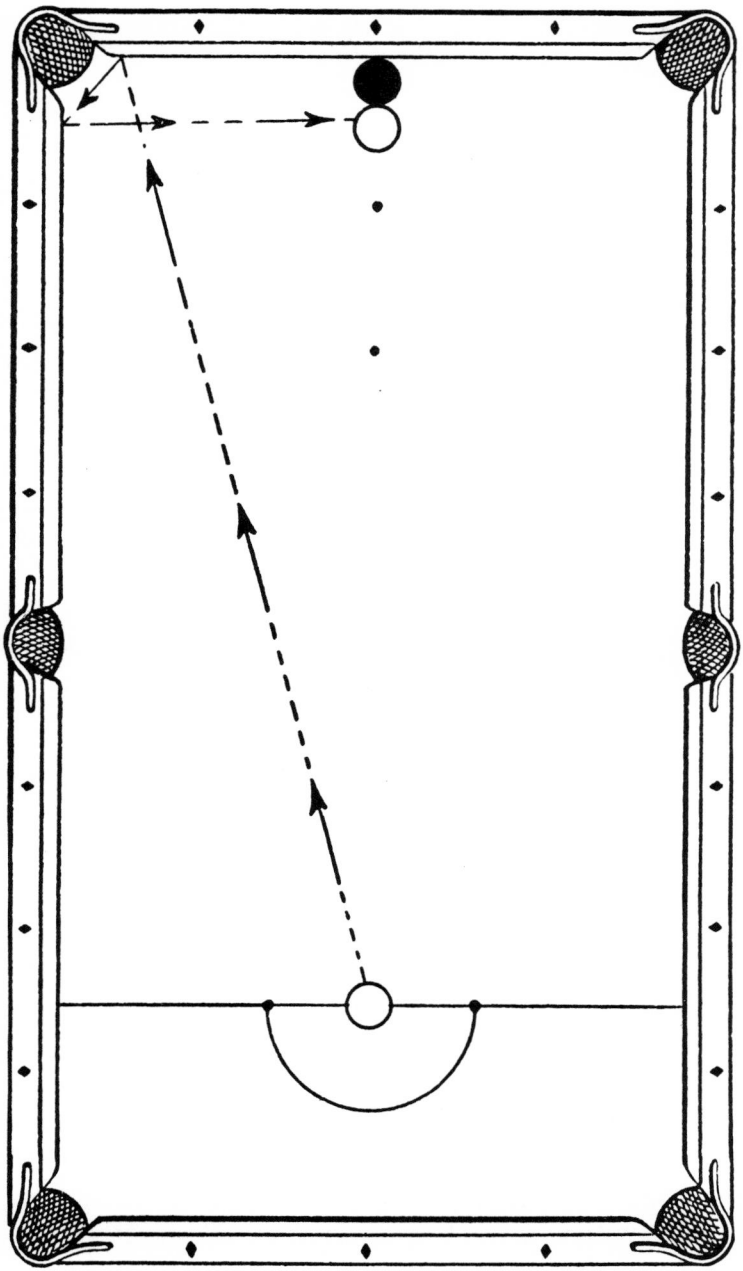

No. 12.

No. 13.

PYRAMIDS: ONE POCKET AGAINST FIVE.

This is an amusing game, and with equal players the odds are also equal. The game is: one player is to have only one pocket, usually the left-hand top corner; the other five belong to his opponent. Each player counts only the balls that go into his own pocket or pockets, no matter who puts them in. The player who takes the one pocket has the privilege of starting, his object being to get a ball over his pocket. The scheme for the player who takes the five pockets is to get all the balls down the table as quickly as possible. The one-pocket player should never try to take a ball hard unless he is certain of it, but should leave it over the pocket if it does not go in.

No. 14.

RUN A BALL OFF TWO CUES.

Place two cues on the table with the tips underneath a cushion and place a ball on them, as in illustration. The trick is to make the ball roll off the cues at the butts without letting the ball touch the table.

For example: Open the cues very gently and slightly until the ball commences to roll toward you. Get up as much speed as you can on the ball, then close the cues. If you do this at the right second, the ball will have sufficient way on it to roll up and over the ends. If not, it will run back again to the cushion.

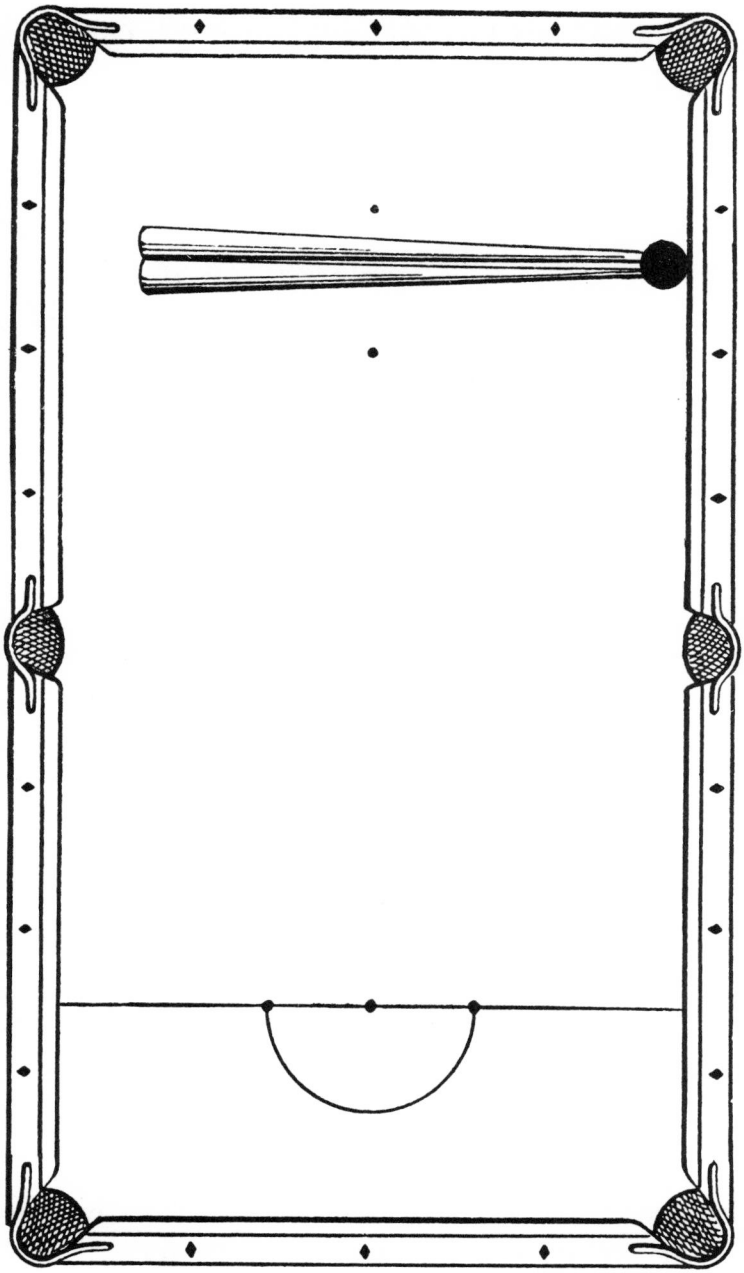

No. 14.

No. 15.

HOW TO KNOCK A SMALL COIN FROM UNDER THE CUSHION.

If a quarter is placed on its edge under the cushion at the spot marked A in the illustration, and the ball played from balk, it will be found extremely difficult to dislodge the coin, unless you are aware of the secret. If you ask any one not acquainted with the trick to do it, he will invariably strike the cushion exactly over the coin, as shown by the dotted lines in the diagram, but the ball will always rebound off the cushion, leaving the coin unmoved. The only way to accomplish the trick is to strike the cushion very slightly beyond the coin, following the course of the firm lines in diagram. If this is done the middle of the ball, which, being the widest part, goes slightly under the cushion, will just catch the edge of the coin and send it spinning.

No. 16.

QUARTER IN THE POCKET.

Lean a quarter up against a side cushion about six inches from the bottom pocket, then take aim at the quarter with the tip of the cue, at the top pocket on the same side. Hit the quarter a smartish tap, and if struck correctly, after a few graceful curves it will drop into the top pocket.

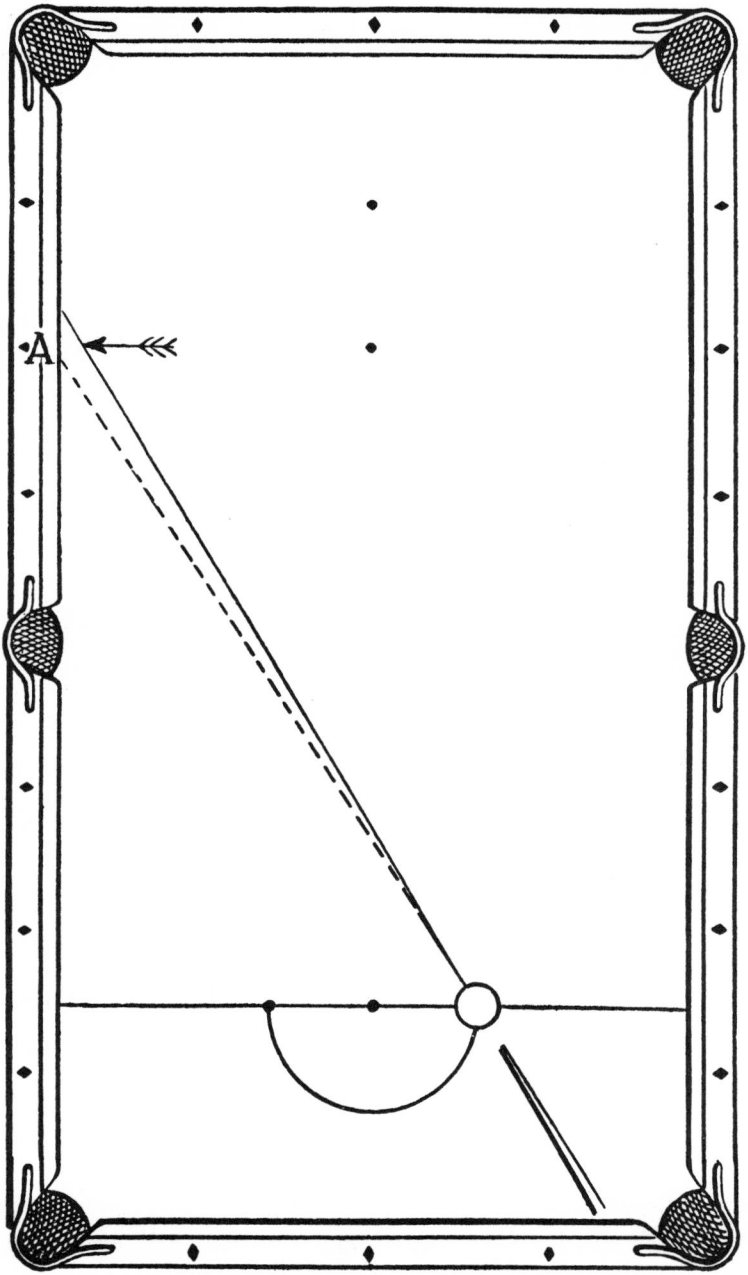

No. 15.

No. 17.

STEEPLE-CHASE SHOT.

There are several games on the billiard and pool table in which the knowledge of how to make one ball jump over another is extremely useful, but the fear of cutting the cloth deters many from making the attempt. It can be done in the following manner, and the cloth cannot be cut. Lay the cue full length on the table, then take the butt into the hand, holding it in the usual way, but so that the butt is not more than three inches away from the table. Place the first and second finger of the other hand over the cue near the tip, as though you were playing a ball through your fingers on the cushion. On no account raise the tip from the cloth, but drag it backward and forward along the cloth, in addressing the ball in the usual way. Hit moderately hard, depending of course on the distance you want to jump. If you hit your ball truly in the middle you can jump it perfectly straight. Of course this shot cannot be done if you are near a cushion.

No. 18.

TO POCKET A BALL THROUGH MATCH BOXES.

Get two outside covers of any sort of the ordinary match boxes, large size. Place them on the pool table with a ball on each. Put a third ball in a line with a pocket and the two other balls as in illustration. Play a hard shot with the ball on the table into the pocket through the match boxes, which should fly off the table, and the two balls will occupy the places where the match boxes stood.

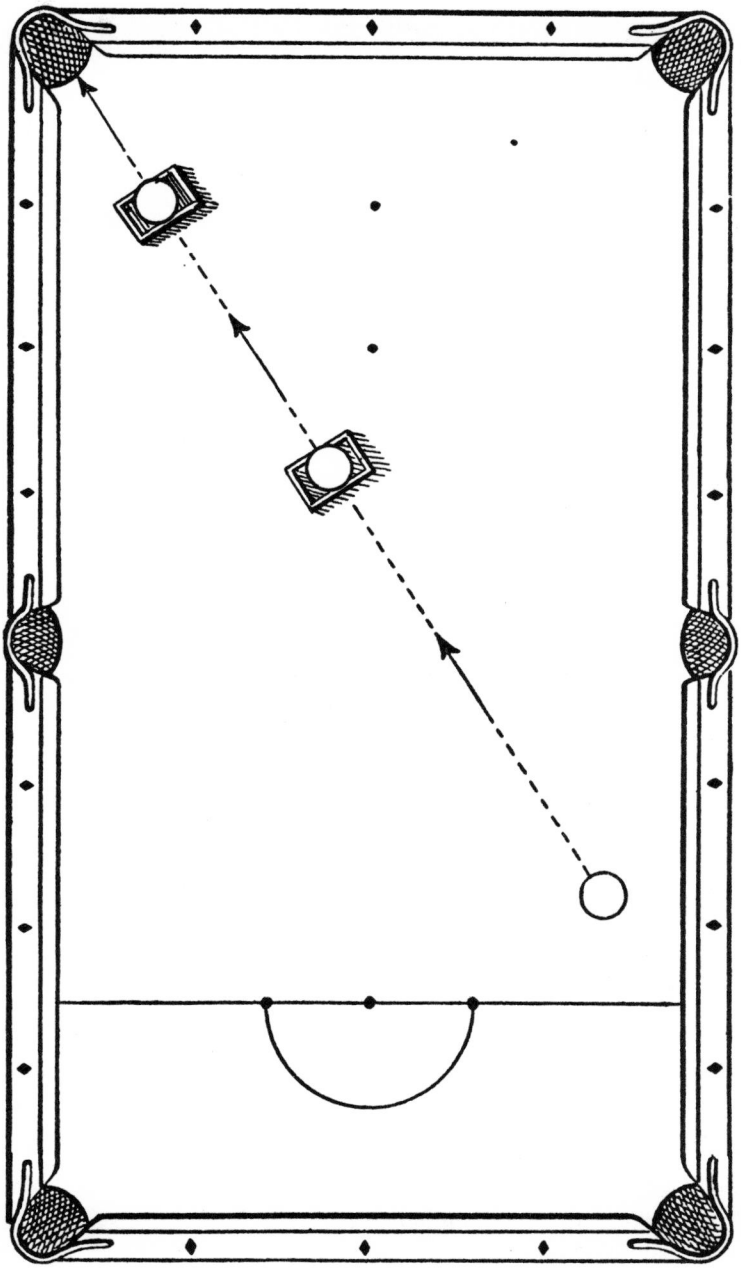

No. 18.

No. 19.

DECEPTIVE POCKET SHOT.

Place three balls in the middle of the table as in illustration. The trick is to play with a ball farthest from the red, and to pocket the red in the middle pocket. This is a trick in which the quickness of the hand has to deceive the eye. For example: Take up your position as though you were going to hit the ball in the usual way, but in reality don't look at the white ball at all. Keep your eye fixed on the red. Then with a very quick shot, push through the white ball, which will slightly separate and allow the tip of your cue to go through and hit the red and drive it into the pocket. If done very quickly it cannot be perceived. Try it slowly first to get the idea.

No. 20.

PASS THROUGH.

HAND SHOT.

Jamb two balls into a corner pocket perfectly squarely, and place a third ball tight up against the middle of them, touching both balls. The shot is to hit the ball farthest from the pocket and make it pass through the middle of the two other balls into the pocket. For example: Make a straight, sweeping shot with the palm of the hand at the top of the outside ball, straight at the middle of the pocket. If hit correctly the two inside balls will run away carrying the ball you hit with them about a foot, but the "English" you have put on your ball with the blow will cause it to run back again into the pocket.

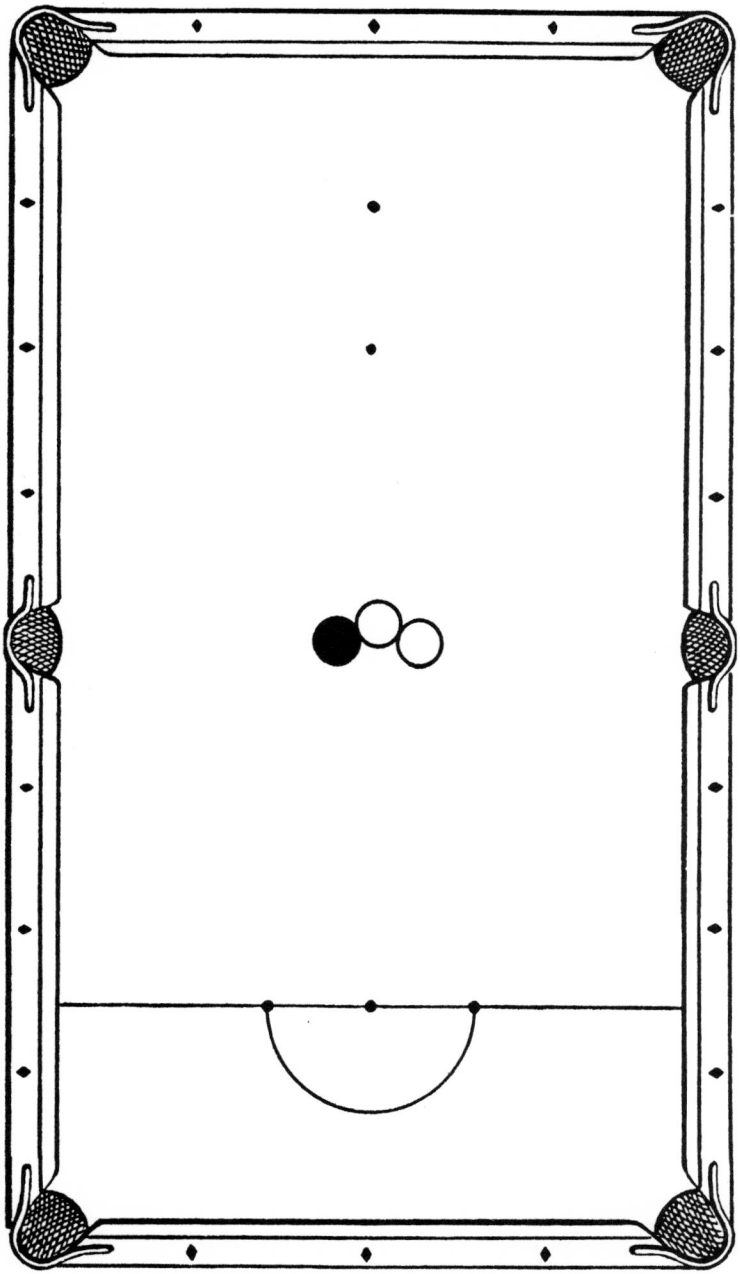

No. 19.

No. 21.

A PRETTY CAROM.

Arrange two cues, with the butt ends in the jaw of the top left-hand pocket, and place a ball on the top of them so that they will be jammed firmly in the pocket; they will then form a V with the thick ends touching. The ball on the top will then be fixed, and cannot be knocked into the pocket or run down cues. Now place the red ball midway between the open ends. To make the shot, play from balk, and, striking your ball rather high, hit the first cue about eighteen inches from its tip; the ball will then jump over the cue, and though not having enough strength to jump the second cue, it will be found that the ball has just sufficient impetus to reach the white ball at the butt end of the cues. After touching this, it will start to run down the incline, and, leaving the cues, it will run straight on to the red, getting the carom.

No. 22.

SQUEEZE SHOT.

A useful shot to know, playing the old rules, but is barred by the new ones. Place the red ball, touching a cushion, about fourteen to eighteen inches from a corner pocket and place a white ball, almost touching it, as in illustration. The shot is to pocket the red in the nearest pocket.

For example: Push the white up against the red and squeeze them against the cushion; hang on to it until both balls commence to run toward the pocket, then let go. The red should kiss in off the white into the pocket, although it frequently goes in straight.

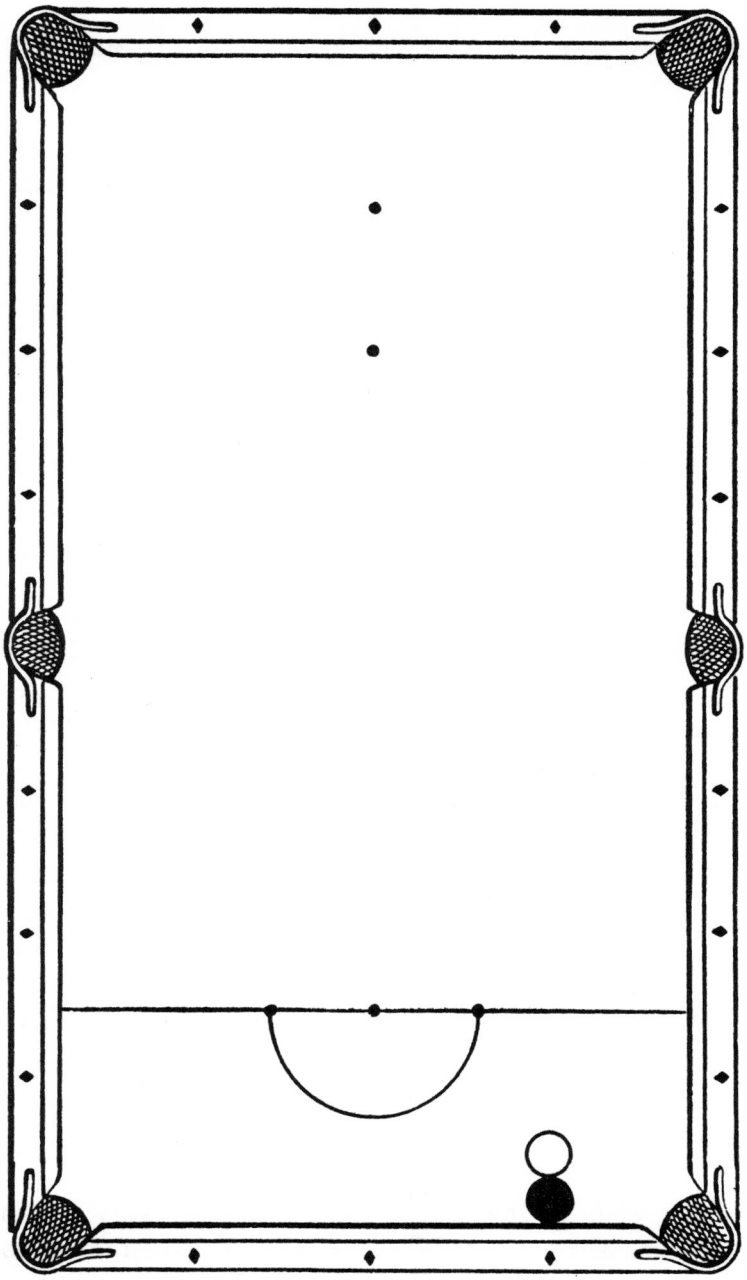

No. 22.

No. 23.

TO POCKET THREE BALLS IN SAME MIDDLE POCKET IN TWO SHOTS.

Place two balls just in front of the middle pocket as in illustration, and another ball on the right hand spot of the D. The trick is to play with a ball from balk and to pocket the three balls in the middle pocket in two shots.

For example: Aim the ball you play with straight into the middle pocket without touching the other two—of course you must just leave room for this—and then play the other two into the pocket, playing with the outer ball.

No. 24.

A NEW STROKE.

This is a peculiar way of getting a carom, but it is invariably successful. Place one white ball and the red side by side on the balk line touching the cushion, the other white ball is touching the opposite cushion, so that the three balls are now in a straight line. This shot can be only got with a flexible cue, which is held against the side of the white ball, the right hand being in the usual position at the butt. Press the ball tightly against the cushion with the cue, at about twenty-four inches from its tip, then drawing the cue toward you sharply, still pressing the ball, cause the ball to run up the table. This movement, which is very difficult to describe, is somewhat on the same principle as squeezing an orange pip from the fingers. The ball will then travel up to the top cushion, and will be found to have a lot of running side on it which will take it at a sharp angle off the cushion and get a carom.

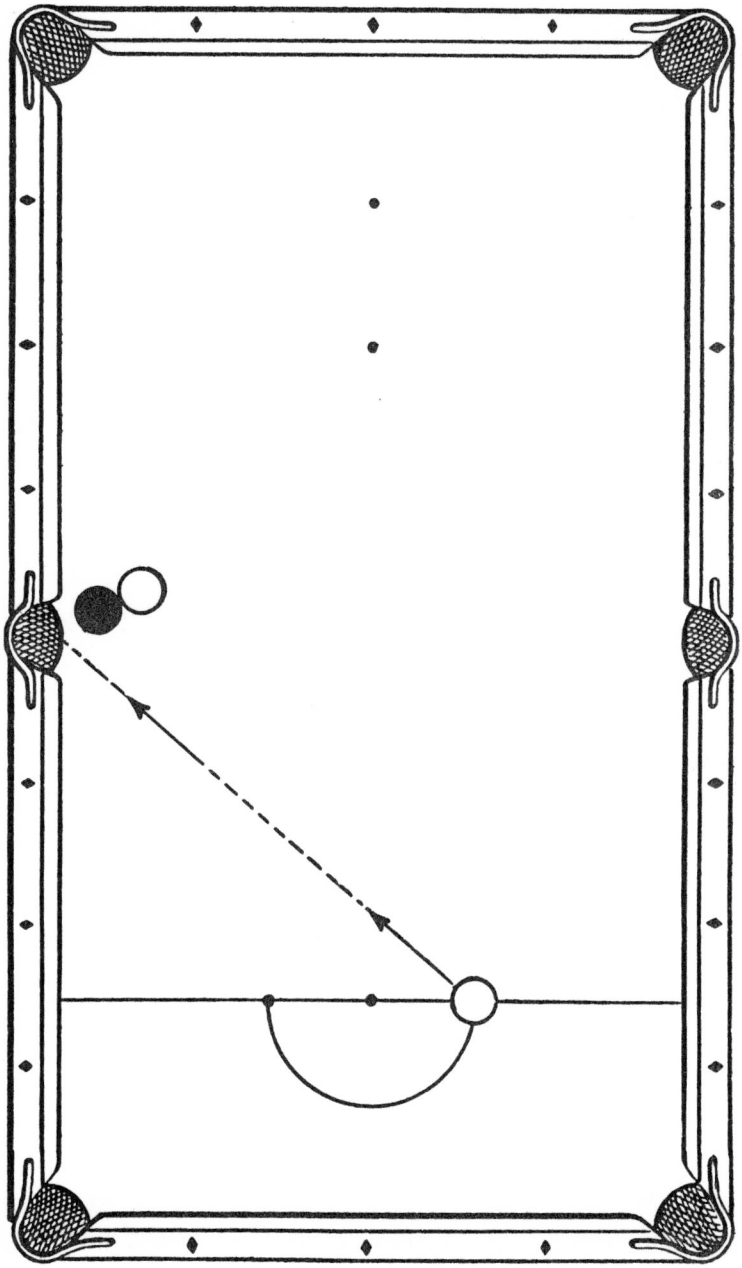

No. 23.

No. 25.

TRICK HAND CAROM.

The following is a very deceptive hand carom shot and should be done quickly and neatly or the trick is given away.

Place the balls up against the cushions as in illustration. The trick is to make a hand carom from the red to the white on the other side of the table. It is a trick you might try forever if you hit the red ball first. For example: Sway the palm of the hand backward and forward over the white and red balls, then make a sweeping stroke over the red with the palm of the hand as though you were going to hit the red, but don't do it, just miss it, and hit the white, which will drive the red across the table and hit the opposite white —that is, if you have put all three in a straight line. It can also be done the whole length of the table.

No. 26.

THE HATCHET STROKE.

Balance a ball on the woodwork of the cushion (it will rest easily and quickly in any little indentation in the wood). The trick is to knock the ball on to the table with the hand in such a manner that it does not go eighteen inches away from the cushion.

For example: Strike the ball a fairly hard blow with the edge of the hand (as if the hand were a hatchet) about half ball. This will put on check as though the ball were screwed back, and the ball will either stop dead or it will frequently run back to the cushion.

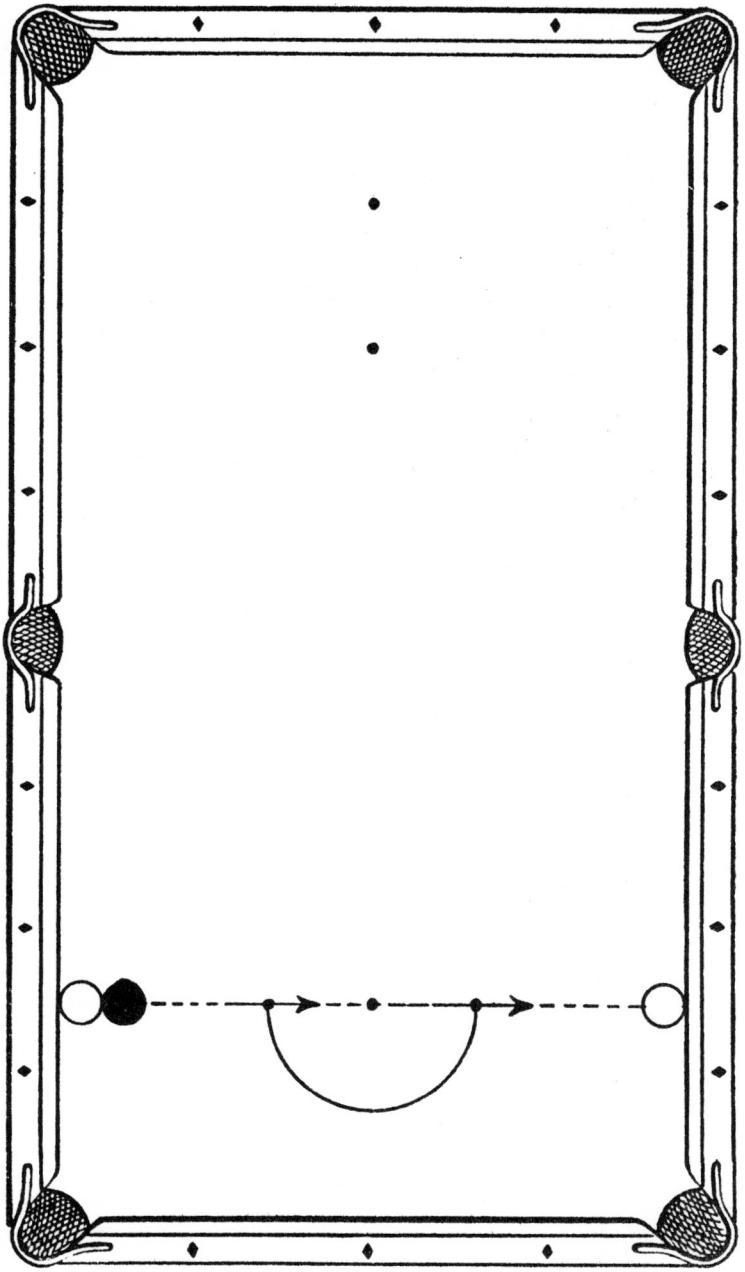

No. 25.

No. 27.

STRAIGHT AIMING.

To see whether you can aim straight and to improve your play when tucked up under a cushion, try the following:

Place a ball tight up against the middle of the top cushion right behind the billiard spot. Practise aiming the ball from that position into all the pockets of the table; the two top pockets are of course easy, but the middle and bottom pockets require practice. It makes a fairly good competition, seeing who can do it in the fewest strokes. The better the table and balls the easier it is (see illustration).

No. 28.

TO POCKET THREE BALLS IN ONE SHOT.

A Trick.

Please put on your coat before showing this trick.

Place a ball in the very jaws of each of the bottom pockets. Place two cues on the table with each butt touching a ball, and the cues absolutely touching each other their whole length as far as possible. The trick is to play a ball up the table with a cue, hit the top cushion first, then to return, hit the cues and all of the three balls to go into a pocket. For example: Play with sufficient strength at the top cushion that when the ball returns and hits the cues it will jump off the table. While it is travelling drop your cue, hold your coat pocket open, and catch the ball in it as it jumps off the table. The blow on the cues will pocket the other two balls, and you have pocketed the three balls in one shot.

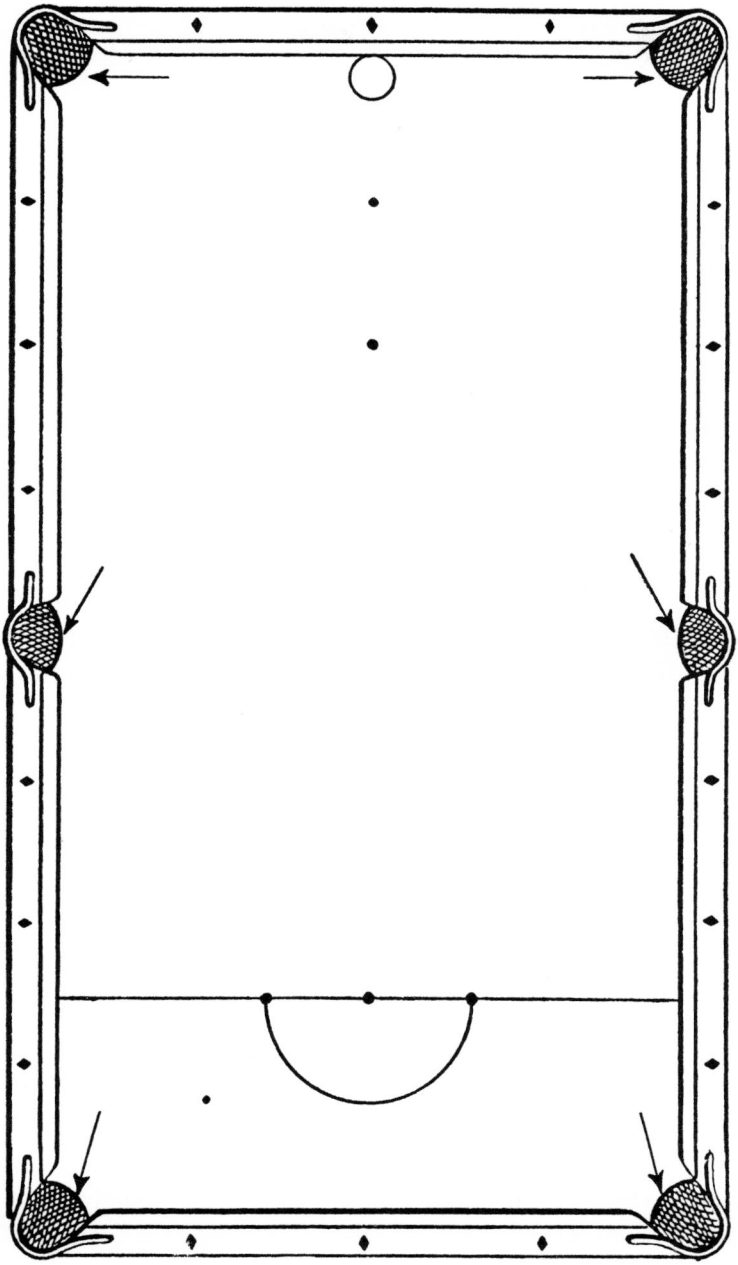

No. 27.

No. 29.

POOL DECK QUOITS.

An amusing game of quoits on the pool or billiard table can be played as follows: Complete the circle D with chalk and make two other rings as shown in the illustration. The game is: You must play from the balk line on either side of the largest ring and hit the top cushion first, and try to bring your ball back into the rings, each of them having different values, your opponent and yourself playing two balls each, tossing for choice of start, which is a disadvantage, as you are liable to have your ball knocked out of the rings. The usual game is eleven points up. A ball is not in if you can see the line underneath it. After hitting the top cushion you may hit any number of other cushions. It can also be played three or more a side with the same rules.

No. 30.

BALK PRACTICE.

The following shot is good practice, and it may help you when you are left a double balk, at the same time it can be played as a competition. Place the red ball touching the middle of the bottom cushion. The game is to pocket the red in the left-hand bottom pocket, starting with a white ball from the D; but every shot played has to be up the table and hit the top cushion first, never direct at the red, even if you have to knock it out of balk. For competition, the one who does it in the fewest number of strokes wins. It has been accomplished in two strokes.

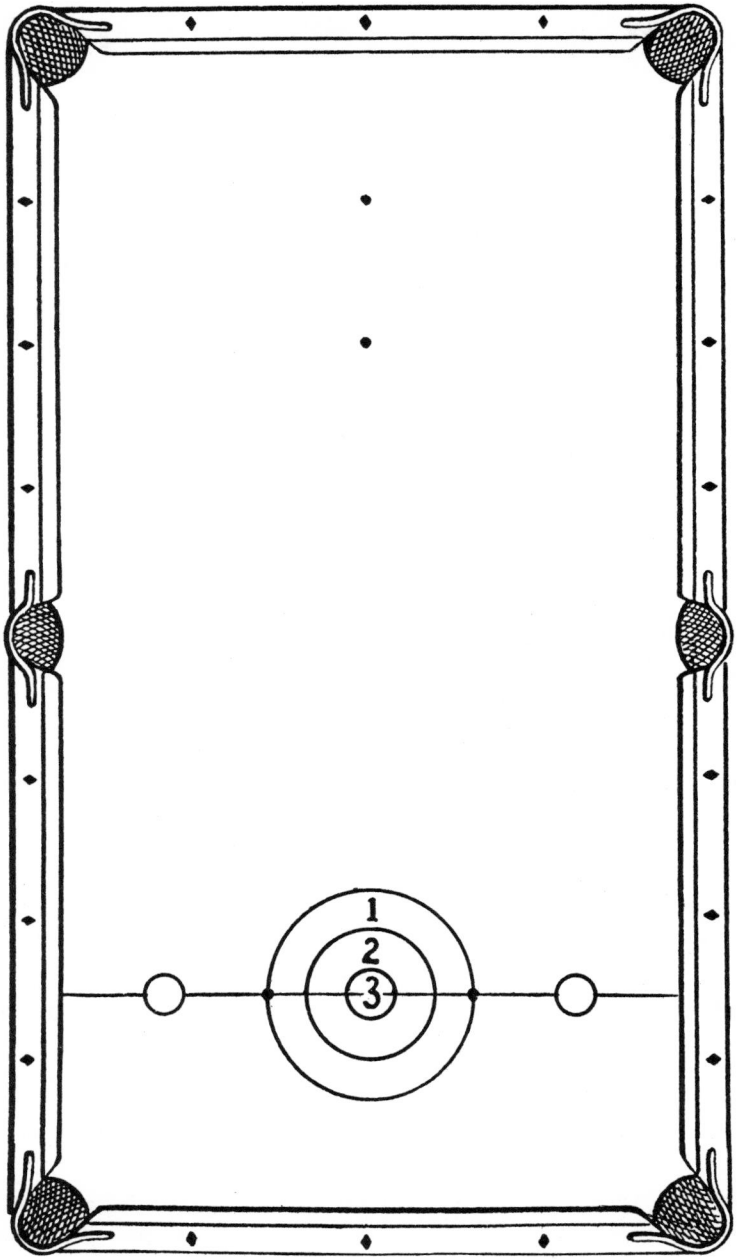

No. 29.

No. 31.

TO POCKET THREE BALLS IN TOP POCKET IN ONE SHOT.

Put a ball into the jaws of each of the top pockets and a third ball on the middle spot of the D. The trick is to pocket the three balls in one shot, playing with the ball in balk. For example: Put two cues on the table as in illustration, but not until after your victim has failed to accomplish the shot. Hit the outside cue with a little left-hand side on your ball, as per dotted lines; the left cue pockets one ball and you are bound to run down the right cue. Hit the ball and follow it into the pocket; not too hard.

No. 32.

CAROMS *VS.* PYRAMIDS.

This is an amusing game, especially with a good hazard-striker, against whom a moderate player ought not to make more than about forty to fifty caroms. Place the pyramid balls on the table in the usual way; one player has to see how many caroms he can make before the other pockets the pyramid balls. For example: The hazard-player plays first from balk, and has a smash at the pyramid. If a ball goes in he continues playing until he fails. Then the carom-player begins. He plays with the white at any two balls he likes; but if his ball is touching another one, or if a ball goes into a pocket whilst he is making his caroms, or if he fails to carom, he has to give way to the pocket player, who goes on until he fails, and so on alternately, until only one pyramid ball is left. With a good hazard-striker not so many caroms are made as one would imagine.

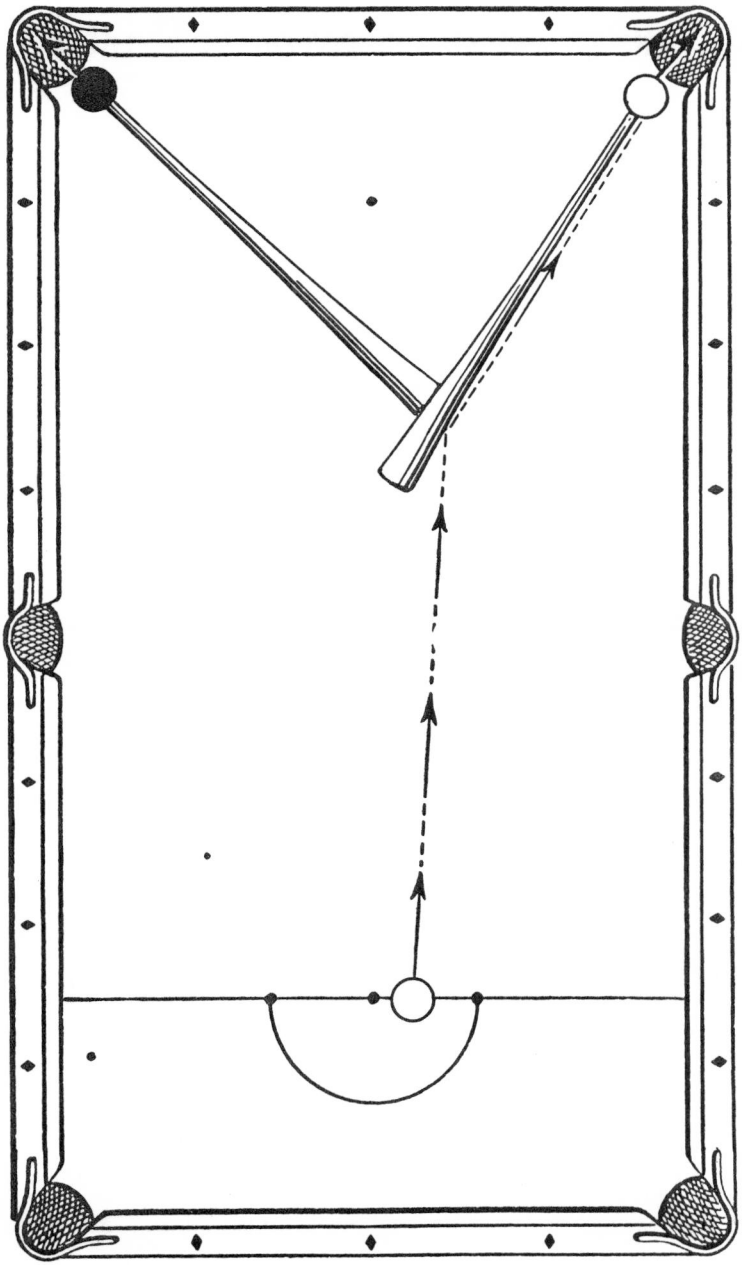

No. 31.

No. 33.

TO POCKET THREE BALLS IN SAME POCKET IN ONE SHOT.

To make this shot nearly every time place the white and red in the jaws of a pocket, the white nearer in than the red, and place another white (the one you are to play with) as in illustration. For example: Play hard at the red, nearly full ball with a lot of "English"; the red will run in and your ball will just touch the white which follows the red, and your ball after running back a little way should follow on into the pocket, if you have put on sufficient "English."

No. 34.

RED INTO BALK TWENTY TIMES.

Place the red on the billiard spot, and play with a ball from balk. You have to play at the red and make it pass the balk line. It doesn't matter if it comes out of balk again, you may safely bet against its performance twenty times in succession, the red being respotted each time. The usual causes of breakdown being playing too full and kissing off the top cushion, or the red catching the bump of a middle pocket. Playing too fine and miscues are also enemies.

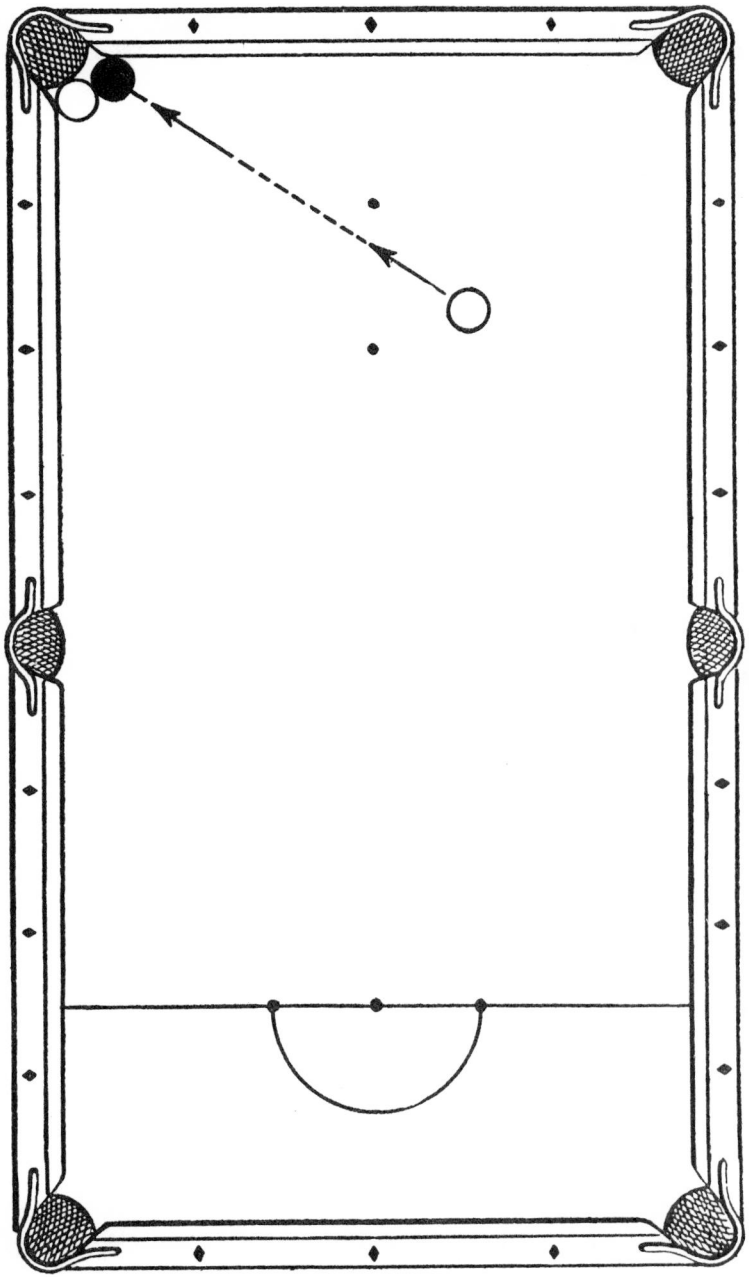

No. 33.

No. 35.

THE WAR GAME.

Any number of players can play this game, the more the merrier; it is quite exciting and provokes great fun. Skill tells, and there is a great element of chance. For example: Place any number of balls on both ends of the table, an equal number on each side, as in illustration. If the skill is greater on one side than the other, you can handicap by giving the weak side a ball or two more. The game consists in bringing the balls from your opponents' end of the table, up to your end, *i.e.*, past the middle pockets. Toss for choice of start, which is an advantage, the winner of the toss electing to let his side play first shot. Then the other side has a shot, and so on alternately until the balls are all on one side of the table or the other. A ball in a pocket is a dead ball. Should a ball be exactly half-way between the pockets you toss for it, and should there be any doubt as to which side a ball belongs you must do the same.

No. 36.

WET CUE TRICK.

This is another trick of the grandfather order.

Put the red ball on the billiard spot and a white ball on the middle spot of the D. Tell your victim he cannot turn round three times, then aim fairly quickly and hit the red ball with the white, you holding his cue whilst he is turning round. No more he will if you wet the tip of his cue with your tongue whilst he is gyrating, only do not let him see you do it.

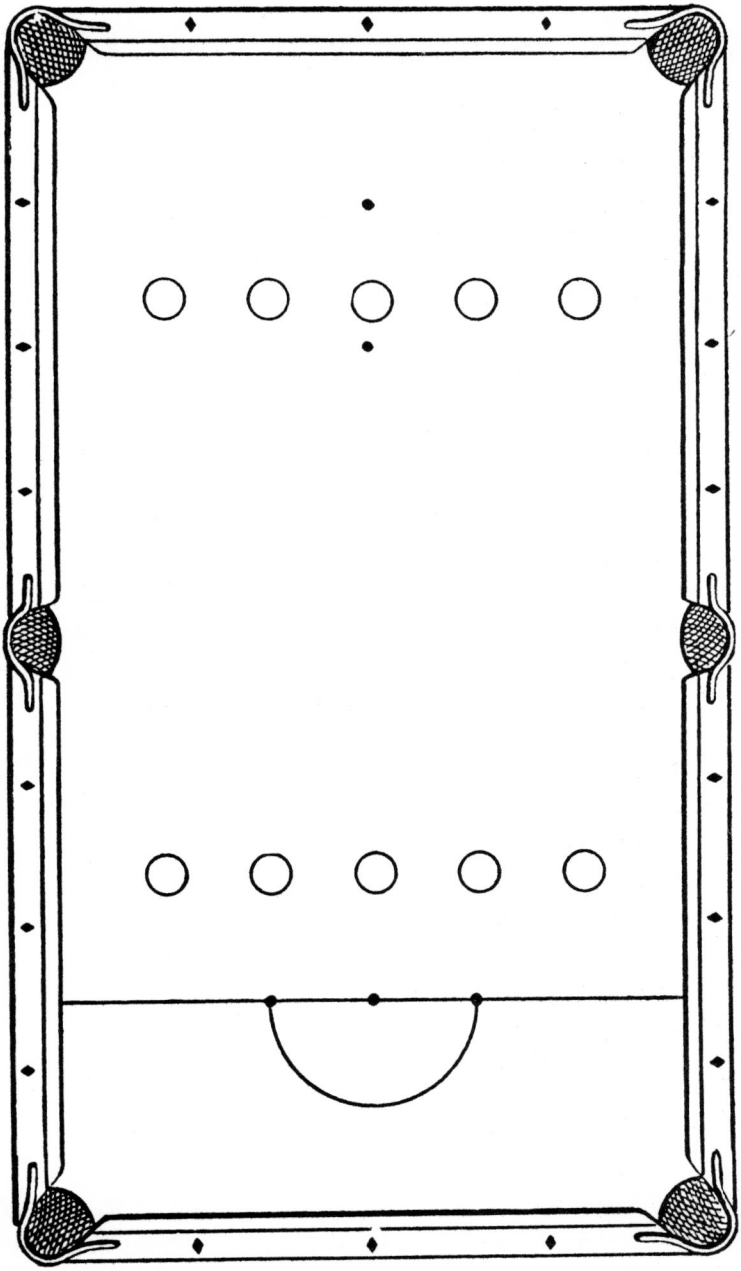

No. 35.

No. 37.

TO POCKET THREE BALLS IN REVERSE ORDER. TOP POCKET.

To pocket three balls in the bottom pocket, sending one round the angles, is baby's play compared to this one. It requires the greatest delicacy of touch and absolute control of the nerves, and without a true table and a good set of balls is very difficult to accomplish. Place the three balls on the spots of the D. The red on the left corner spot, the white on the centre spot, and the spot white on the right spot. You have to hit the red ball first; it has to go into the left-hand top corner pocket last. Hit the white ball second, it has to go into the same pocket second; and play the spot white last, it has to go into the same pocket first. For example: Hit the red ball with only just sufficient strength to reach the pocket. Move quickly to the white and hit it a trifle harder so that it gets just in front of the red, and while these balls are travelling slowly up the table move rapidly to the spot white and send it in with a bang.

No. 38.

TRICKY POCKET SHOT.

Place a white ball on the right-hand spot of the D, and place the red ball just past the middle pocket, touching the cushions, but too far up to be cut in with the white (see illustration). The shot is to pocket the red direct into the middle pocket. For example: Aim at the red ball with the white almost a full ball, favoring the right "English" just a little. Put plenty of right "English" on your ball, and if you hit it just right the red should roll round into the pocket. Rather a slow shot.

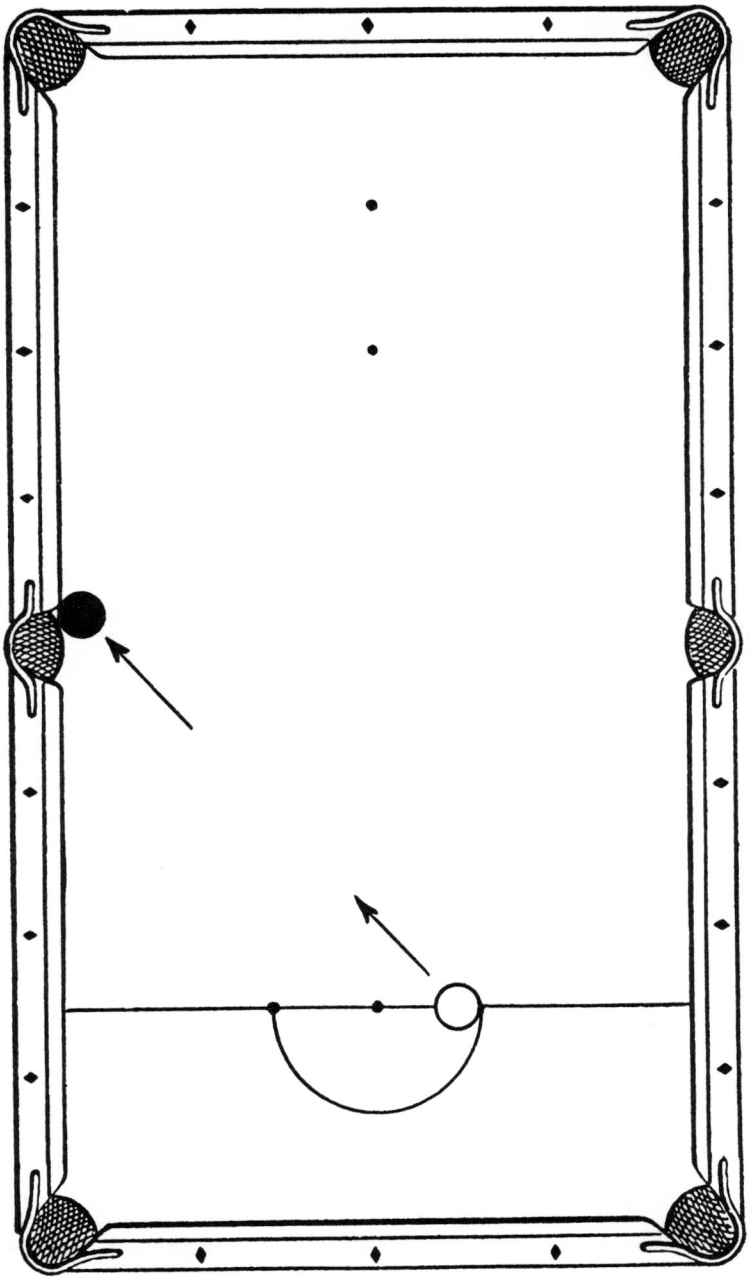

No. 38.

No. 39.

TO GO INTO THE MIDDLE POCKET OFF THE RED WITHOUT MOVING THE WHITE BALL PLACED ON CENTRE SPOT.

This is another shot which is very mystifying until you know how its done. Place the red on the edge of one of the middle pockets, and one of the white balls in the same position over the other middle pocket; then put the other white ball on the centre spot so that all the balls are in a straight line. Now the trick is to go in the middle pocket off the red without moving the other white ball and without pocketing the red. This may be done by striking with your ball the bottom cushion exactly in the centre, when the ball will take an angle so just as to touch the red, and will go into the pocket. No side is required, and to make it more certain, a small chalk mark can be made on the cushion beforehand. This is a very good test to see whether the table and the balls are running true, as it is impossible to miss the shot under ordinary conditions.

No. 40.

TO POCKET THREE BALLS IN ONE SHOT, MIDDLE POCKETS.

Place the red over one middle pocket, the plain white over the other, and the spot white six inches behind the red (see illustration), all three balls being in a straight line. The trick is to play with the spot white and pocket the three balls in one shot in the middle pockets. For example: As you draw back the cue to hit the spot white knock in the plain white with the butt of the cue, and follow on the red into the pocket—a six shot; if done quickly it goes well.

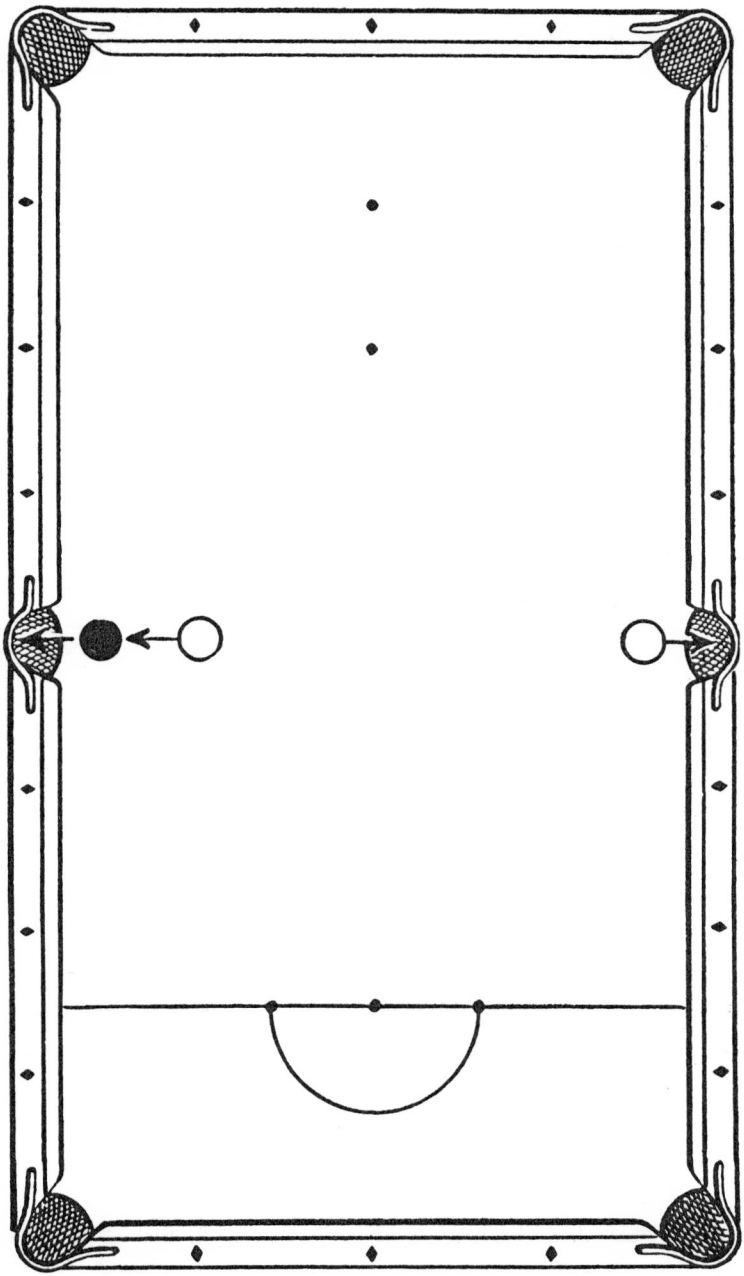

No. 40.

No. 41.

PYRAMID BALLS ALONG A CUSHION.

Place the pyramid balls along the top cushion, draw one back along the cushion about a foot, and play it at the remainder, and one will go into the opposite pocket. Draw two back, make them touch, and then play them both at the remainder, and two will go in, and if you draw back three, make them touch, and then play them, their weight will cause three to go into the opposite pocket.

No. 42.

CAROM THROUGH A HAT.

Place a hat on the table, either a high hat or a derby (a curly brimmed one), the same way as you would on your head, and place two balls about two inches apart two feet from one side, and place the other ball, the one you are to play with, about three feet the other side of the hat, so that the middle of the side of the hat is in an exact line between your ball and the other two (see illustration). The trick is to make a straight carom without taking the hat from the table or jumping over it. For example: Aim with just sufficient strength to reach the two balls, and just as your ball approaches the hat put the tip of your cue underneath the

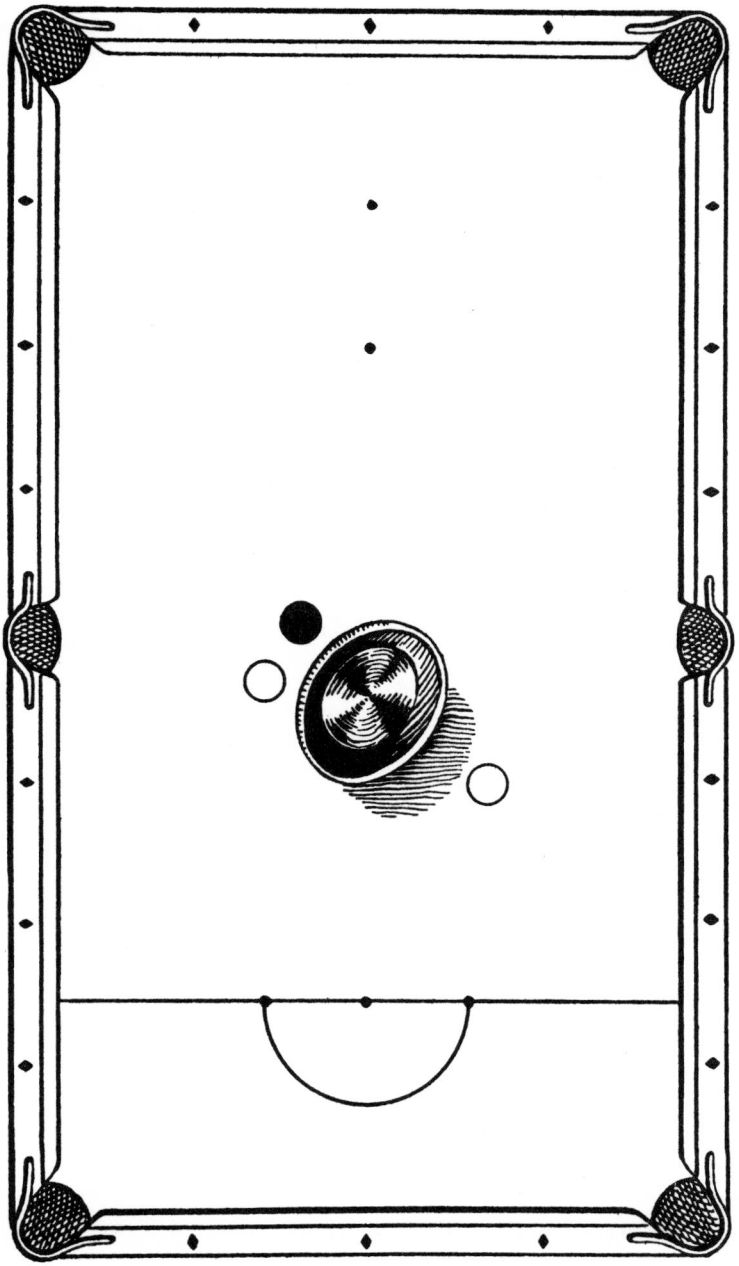

No. 42.

brim on the side nearest to yourself, and tilt the hat well up on the farther brim, just as the ball gets to about the spot where the brim rested let go. The hat will come down and raise itself on the brim nearest to you, and will allow the ball to pass out on the other side and make a carom, the difficulty of course being to let go the hat at the right second.

No. 43.

THREE CUES ON THE TABLE.

The following is an amusing game for a competition as any number can play. It doesn't take long, and is good practice.

Place three cues on the table, as in illustration, put the red on the billiard spot, and a white ball, the one you are to play with, behind it in a straight line with the left-hand top corner pocket. The game is to pocket the red ball in the left-hand bottom corner pocket, playing at it with the white without touching any of the three cues. The one who does it in the fewest strokes wins.

RULES.

A miss counts two.

To go into a pocket a burst—*i.e.*, chance gone.

To pocket the red in a wrong pocket a burst.

To touch any of the three cues with either ball a burst.

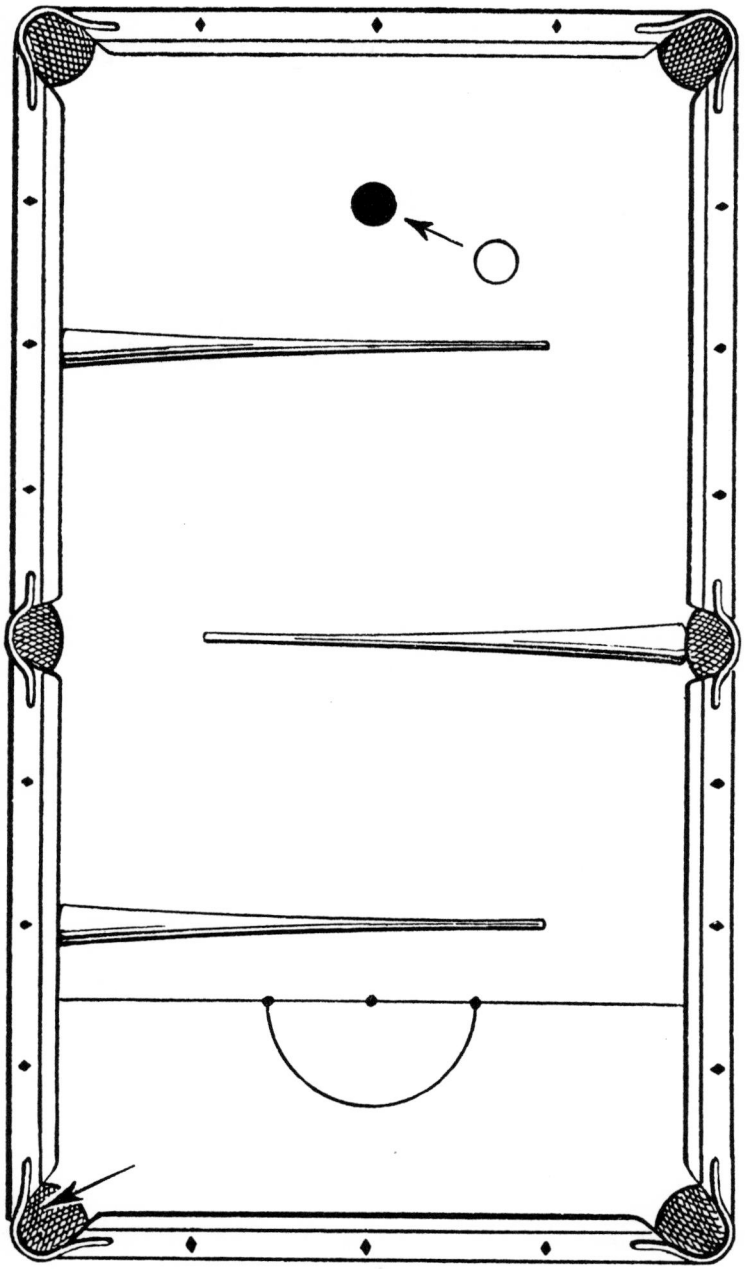

No. 43.

No. 44.

HAND POCKETING COMPETITION.

This is another hard-working game played by two players. The game is to roll a ball by hand into every pocket of the table, two players starting at once, one at the left-hand bottom pocket, the other at the right-hand top corner, so that the two balls have to pass each other. Wait for the word "Go!" and then both start together, care being taken not to scratch the cloth with the nails, nor should the balls be played hard. If your ball goes in you recover it yourself, and go facing the next pocket. If the ball does not go in, you must recover it yourself and try again from the old position. The pockets have to be done in order, moving round to the left till you have done them all. Whichever finishes first wins. (See diagram for order of pockets.)

No. 45.

THE RUNNING SHOT.

An amusing game and one that requires judgment of pace. Place a ball anywhere in the D of balk and get some one to roll a play or ball across the pyramid spot from side cushion to side cushion at a moderate to a hard pace, varying it every time. The game is to hit the ball whilst it is travelling,

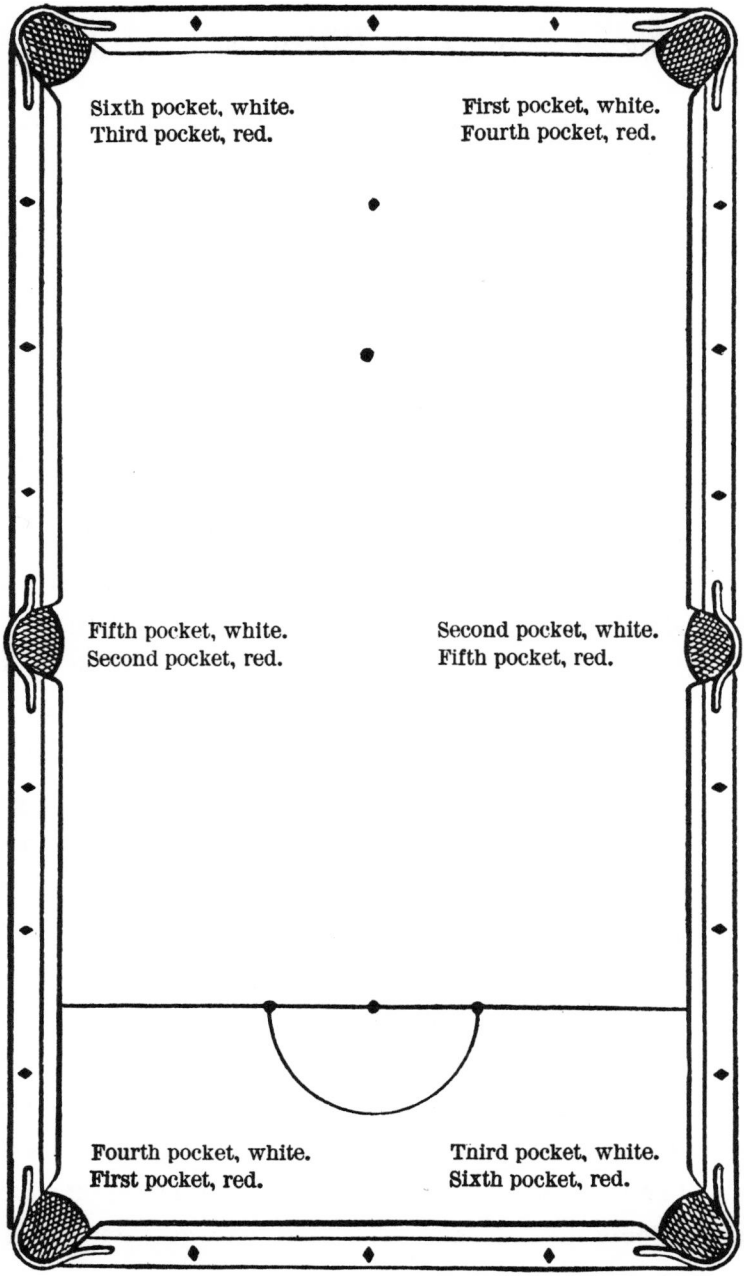
Sixth pocket, white.
Third pocket, red.
First pocket, white.
Fourth pocket, red.
Fifth pocket, white.
Second pocket, red.
Second pocket, white.
Fifth pocket, red.
Fourth pocket, white.
First pocket, red.
Third pocket, white.
Sixth pocket, red.

No. 44.

playing with the ball from balk. As the ball is not always hit or rolled, the same pace judgment has to be used as to when to hit your ball so as to strike the moving ball up the table. The shot should be made as the ball comes back from the first cushion.

No. 46.

TO HIT THE LAST BALL FIRST.

This is a pretty trick, requiring firmness and steadiness of hand and judgment of pace; the number of balls used will depend entirely on the agility and skill of the performer.

Place any number of balls in a straight line, about three to four inches apart, and the ball you are to play with about three feet from the nearest ball. For the purpose of illustration I have put eight balls in the illustration, though a larger number of balls may be used and the trick successfully performed. What you have to do is to play with the solitary ball and hit the farthermost ball, the red, playing in a straight line, without touching an intermediate one, and yet only removing one ball at a time out of the way. For example: Aim at the farthermost ball, the red, with just sufficient strength to reach it, then, with the cue about two inches from the tip and while the ball is travelling knock a ball away with a sweeping stroke right and left alternately, leaving only the last ball. The more strength you use the quicker you have to be.

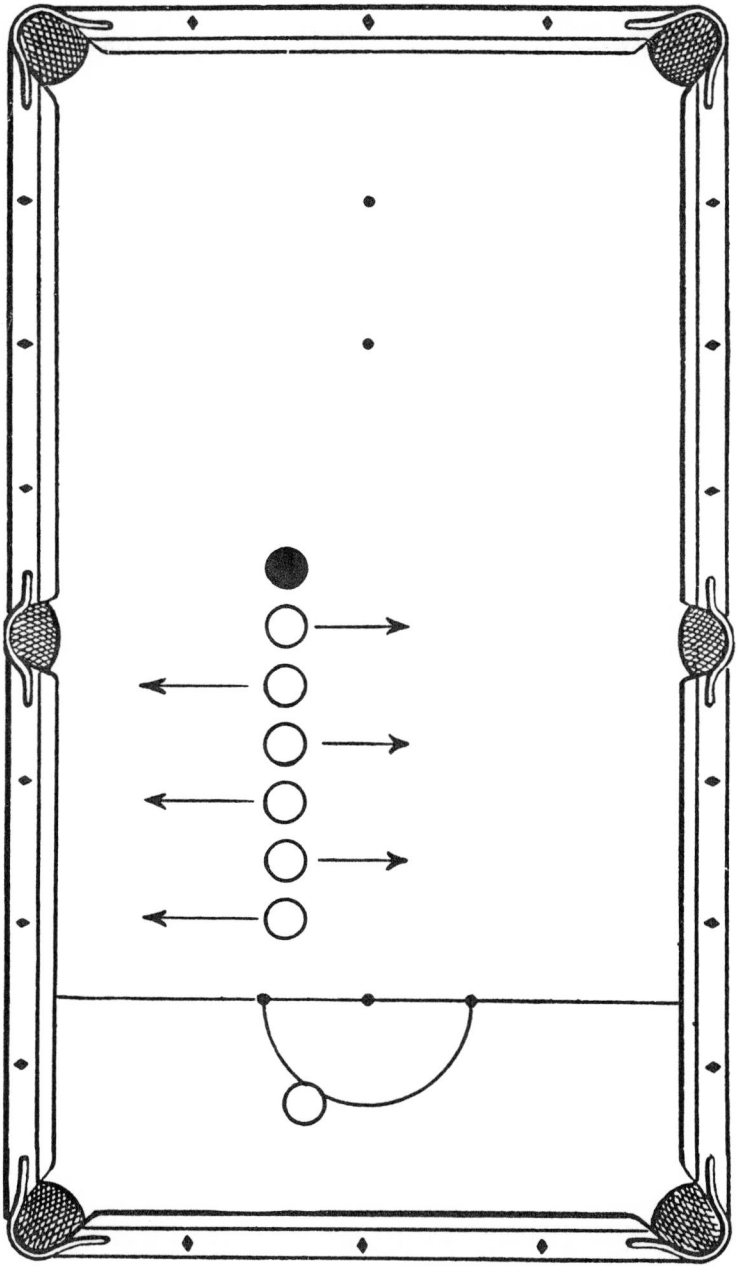

No. 46.

No. 47.

GAME WITH A PLATE ON THE TABLE.

An amusing game which does not take long, full of fun and annoyances.

Place an ordinary dinner plate, face downward, on the pyramid spot as in illustration. The game is to play 15 up as in ordinary pool, but the player who causes any of the three balls to touch the plate while playing his shot, has to wipe off his score and go back to 0. Start the game in the usual way, tossing for choice of start, the winner of toss of course electing to make his opponent play first, as the red is covered for a direct shot. Misses count as usual.

No. 48.

TO RUN A BALANCED BALL ALONG TWO CUES.

Hold two cues of equal size, strongly and steadily side by side in one hand. Place a ball on top of another ball with the other hand, and then put the middle of the two cues lightly on top of the topmost ball. Get the balls balanced by pressing on them with the two cues, and let go the other hand. Then by raising or depressing gently the hand holding them the balls will travel backward and forward, one on top of the other, along the groove made between the two cues.

A steady hand will keep them moving for a considerable time.

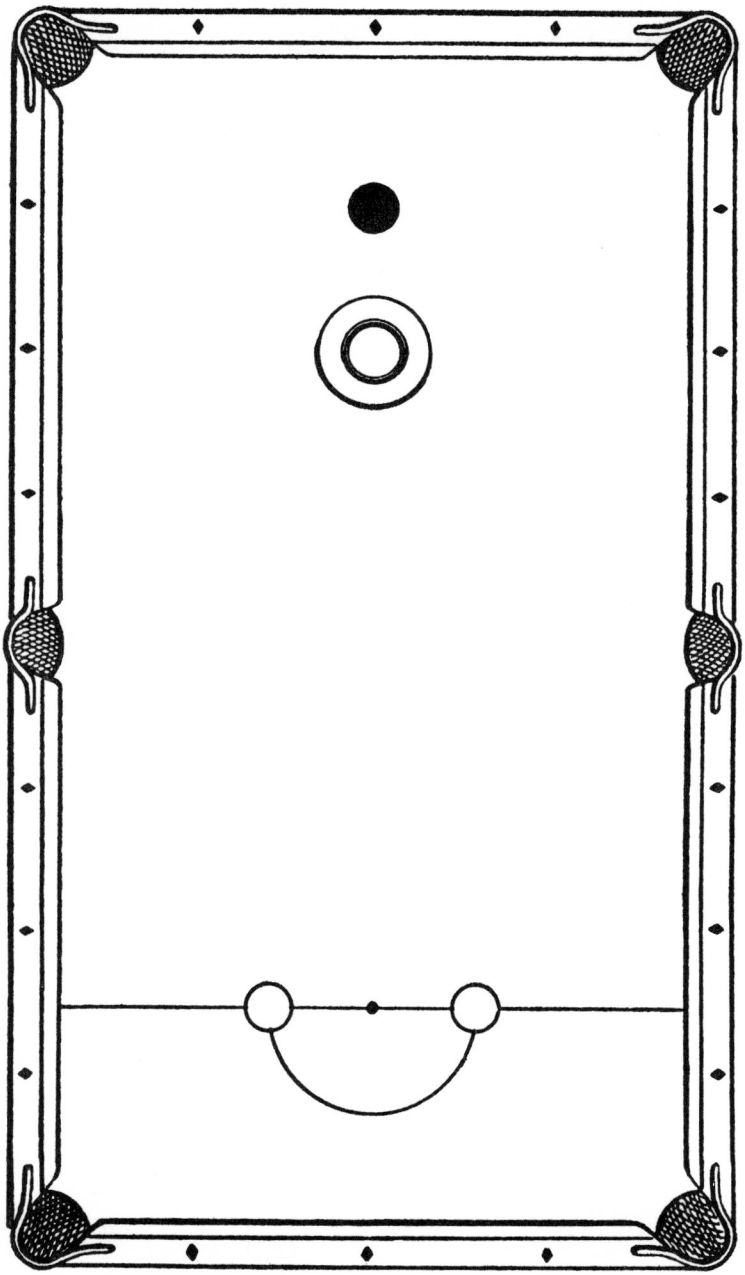

No. 47.

No. 49.

TO POCKET THREE BALLS IN THREE POCKETS IN ONE SHOT.

This is a very effective shot, but great care must be exercised in accurately placing the balls. Place the white a little in front of the middle spot of the D, with the red ball touching it, in a direct line with the outside bump of the left middle pocket, *i.e.*, about three inches above centre of pocket. Place a third ball a little in front of the right-hand bottom pocket as in illustration. The shot is to play with the solitary ball at the other two and send a ball into each of the pockets on the left-hand side.

For example: Go in off the white slowly into the left-hand top corner pocket; the white should kiss off into the left-hand bottom pocket, and the red from the blow should travel into the middle.

No. 50.

SOLITAIRE, OR TABLE GOLF.

Without doubt this is the finest game to play by one's self. It teaches strength, angles, position, caution, and winning hazards; is amusing and makes a good round game, not taking too long. Place the red on the spot in the middle of the table. The game is to pocket it in every pocket of the table in order, commencing with the left-hand top corner pocket

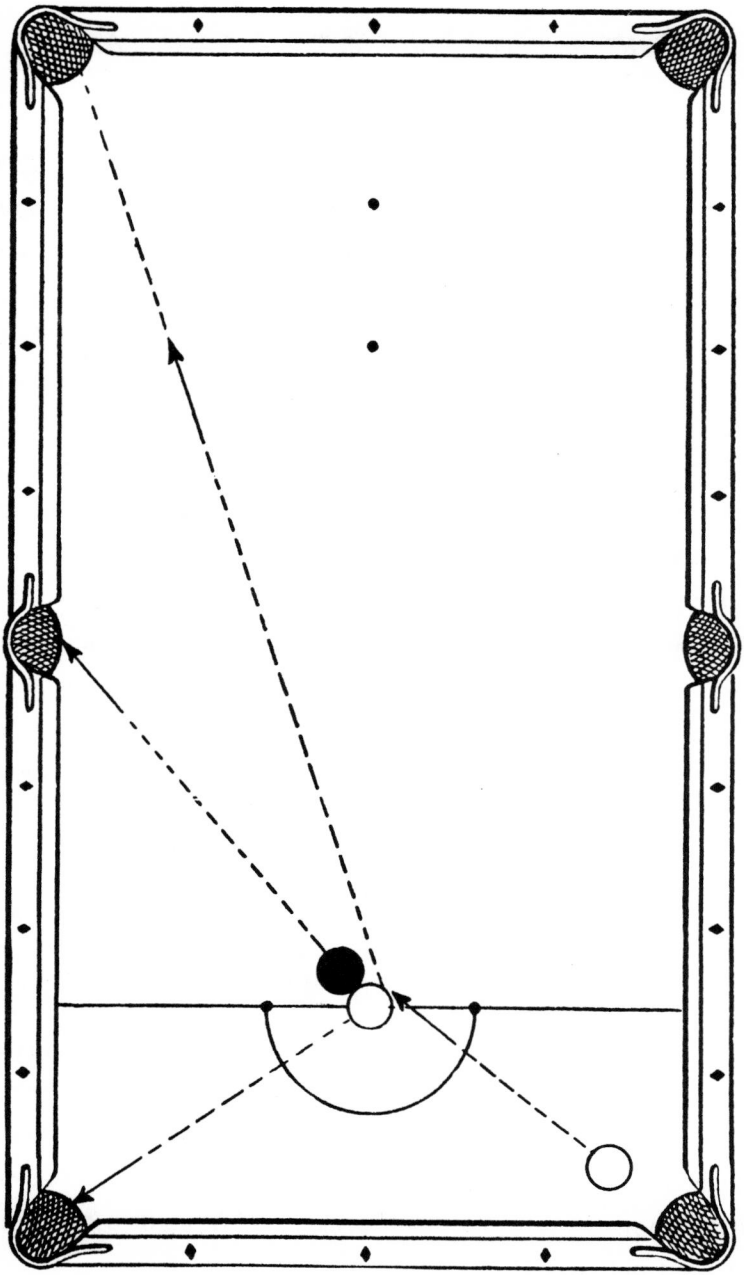

No. 49.

and working round to the right, finishing at the left-hand middle pocket. You play with a white ball, starting from balk. The red is replaced on the middle spot each time after being pocketed, but the white ball is played from wherever it stops. The rules for a competition are: A miss counts two; if the white ball goes into a pocket it is a burst, *i.e.*, your chance is over; if the red ball goes into a wrong pocket—a burst. It can also be played spotting the red on the billiard spot, but is about three strokes more difficult; or it can be played three times round the table, making an eighteen-hole course as in golf. If there are a number of players waiting their turn, it is well to put a limit to the number of strokes each player may make before being compelled to retire. If once around, say sixteen shots; making the limit more or less according to the calibre of the players. Of course the one who does it in the fewest number of shots wins. You can also bring good and bad players together by allowing a few shots.

No. 51.

KISS IN OFF.

Place a red ball tight up against the top cushion. Place a ball in balk as in illustration. The shot is to go in off into a top pocket. For example: Hit the red a little more than three-quarter ball. To go into the right pocket, put on left "English"; to go into left pocket, put on right "English." It need not be played very hard.

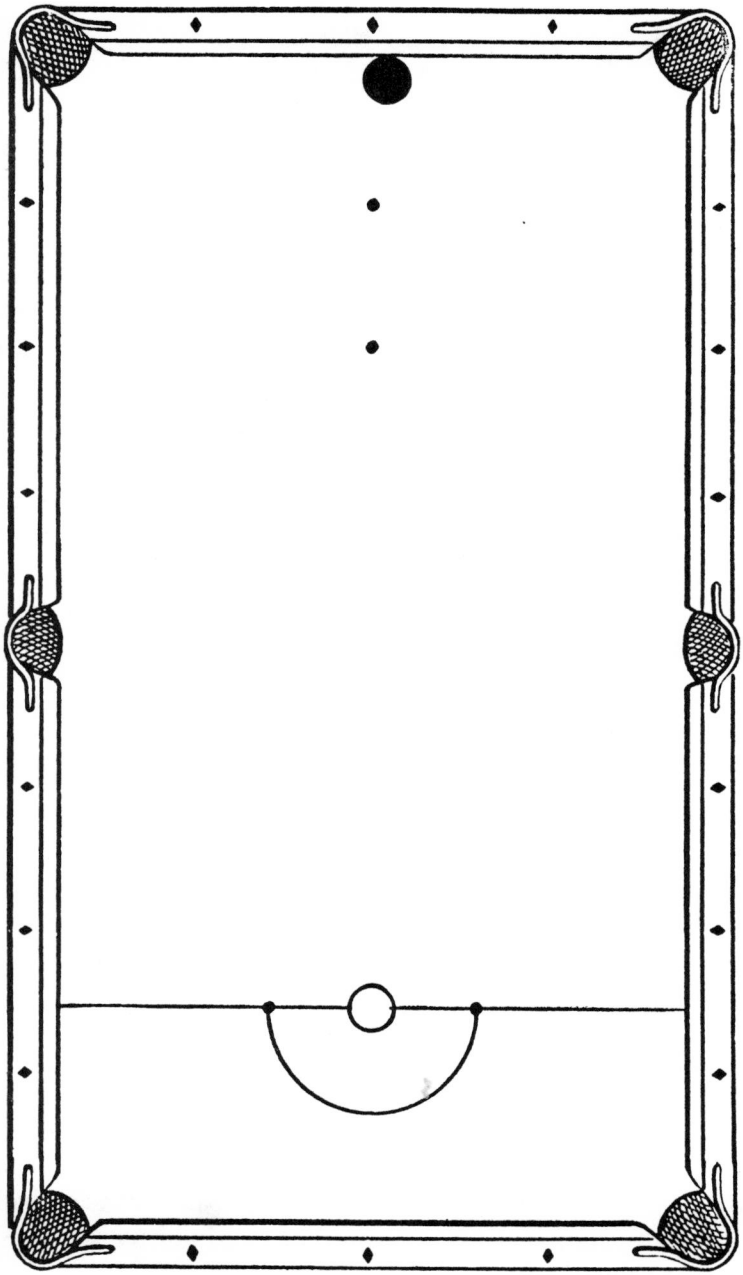

No. 51.

No. 52.

TO CAROM WITHOUT TOUCHING A BALL.

To carom without touching a ball or blowing it along of course seems an impossibility, but when you know how to do it, it is very simple. Place a red and white ball close together, and another ball close to them in position for the simplest of all possible caroms (see illustration). The trick is to carom with the outer ball without touching or blowing the ball. Impossible. Not so. For example: Take a pin, raise the cloth slightly behind the white outer ball, it will roll and make a carom and you haven't touched it. How simple. This will not injure the cloth.

No. 53.

THE LUNG TEST.

To try whether you have really good lungs, place two cues together on the table, with their butts resting up against a cushion, and place a ball on the two cues, down by the tips. If you have good lungs, you will be able to blow the ball up on the cues, and make it touch the cushion. It is easier to do this with a succession of short, jerky puffs, rather than a steady, hard blow.

No. 54.

CAROM TWO CORKS.

Place two corks on the table, the distance between them to be a trifle less than the size of the ball. Place a ball fairly opposite the space between the corks, and try to carom the two corks—a direct carom. Very disappointing.

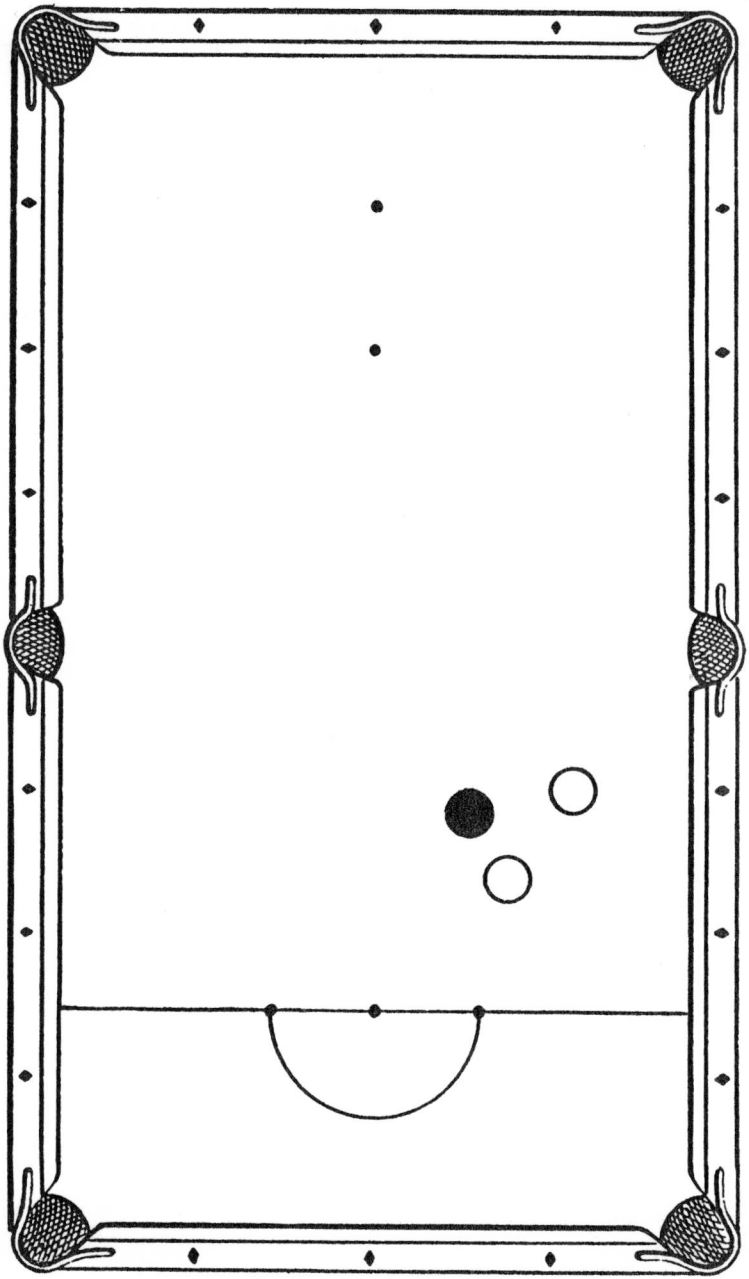

No. 52.

No. 55.

TO POCKET THREE BALLS IN REVERSE ORDER.

BOTTOM POCKET.

This trick requires quickness and self-control. Place the three balls one on each spot of the D, as in illustration, the white on the left-hand spot, the red on the middle, and the spot white on the right-hand spot. The trick is to pocket all three balls in the left-hand corner pocket in balk, in the reverse order of hitting. You have to hit the spot white first, and it has to go into the pocket last, the red second, and it has to go in second, and the plain last, and it has to go in first. For example: Send the spot white round the angles (see line in illustration), then move quickly to the right side of the table, hit the red just sufficiently hard to reach the pocket, then hit the plain white and send it in quickly, passing the red. By the time the plain white is in, followed by the red, the spot white should have gone round the table, and if you have found your angle correctly, should drop into the pocket last.

No. 56.

CAROM LENGTH OF THE TABLE.

Place two balls absolutely touching each other tight up against the top cushion. Play with a ball about a foot away from the bottom cushion and make a carom. If you do not hit the balls accurately between the two, your ball will kiss off, which happens quite as frequently (with moderate players) as the carom is made.

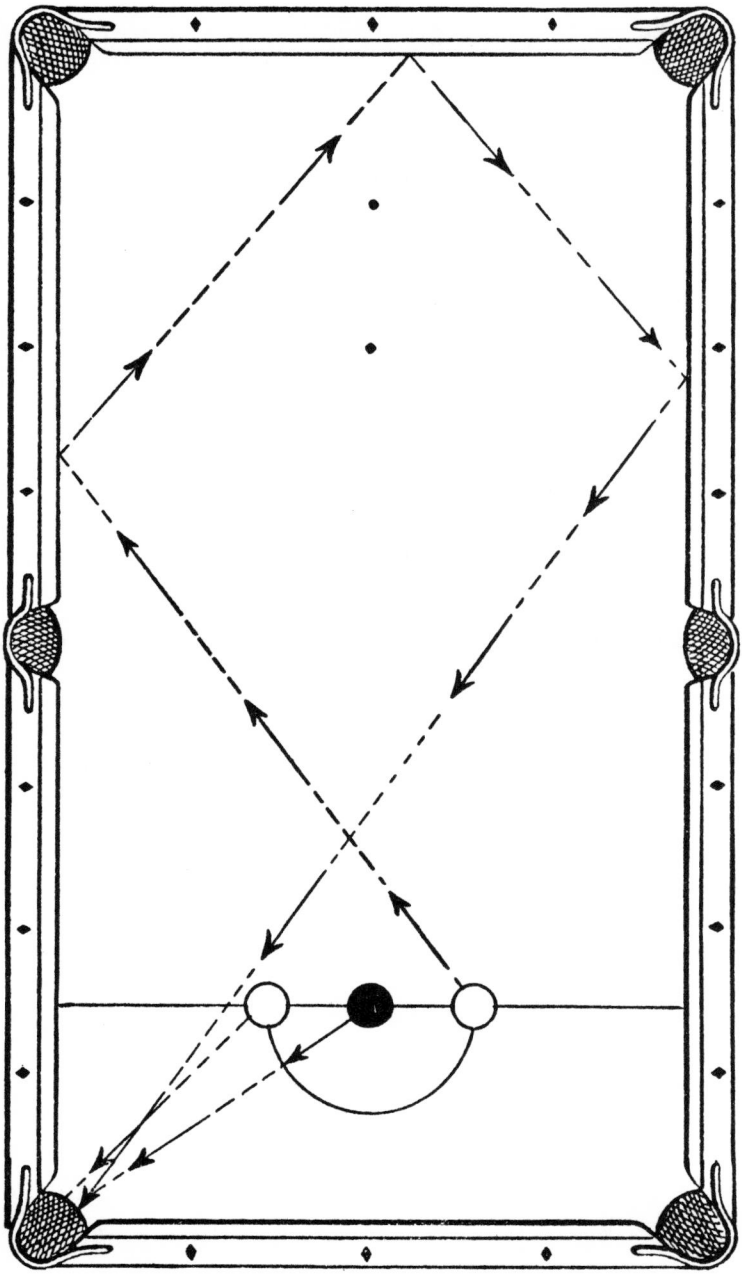

No. 55.

No. 57.

CAROM INTO A HAT.

Place a red ball against the top cushion and a white ball about eighteen inches a little to one side of it, and a hat with a white ball in it about eighteen inches to the other side of it, as in illustration. Play with the white ball at the red, hitting it a little to the right of the centre. Hit down at the ball you play with a fairly hard shot, and as soon as your ball hits the red it should jump into the hat. In hitting down at the white the butt of the cue should be about level with the top of the shoulder.

No. 58.

STEADY HANDS WANTED.

Place an ordinary square of billiard chalk on the table about a foot from one of the side cushions. Take a cue in each hand and from the opposite side of the table try to lift up the chalk with the tips of the cues and place it on the cushion. It is easy if you hold both cues with both hands; if only one hand touches each cue it is very difficult.

No. 59.

STOP SPINNING BALL

Rather an amusing trick is to get some one with strong fingers who can spin a ball well to spin one on the table and then you try to stop it dead by placing one finger on top of it. If it is spinning hard it is difficult. It cannot be stopped by placing the side of a cue on it. Try.

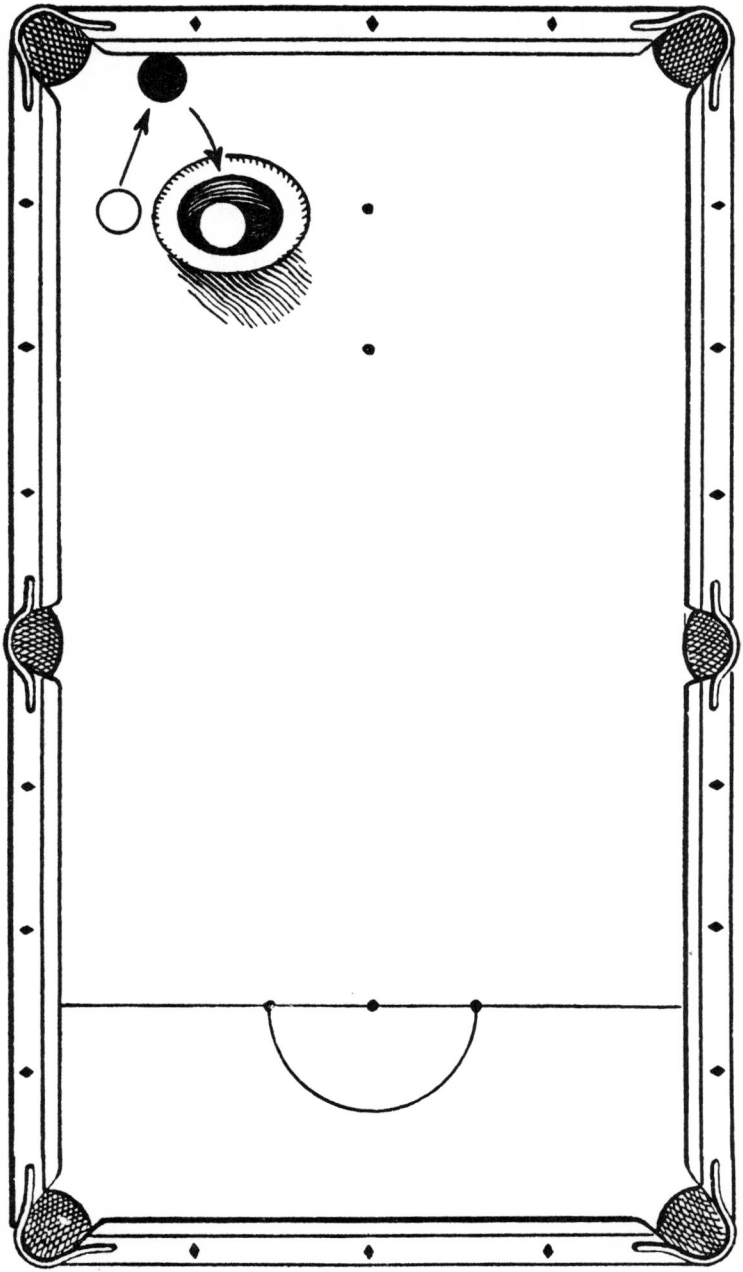

No. 57.

No. 60.

KNOCK DOWN A MATCH.

Make a match stand up upon the billiard spot, and place two balls, which must touch each other, in front of it, as in illustration. The trick is to play from balk with another ball and knock down the match, of course without the aid of the cushion. It is never very easy, but the way it comes off most frequently is to "follow" through one ball with a lot of "English": left "English" for the right-hand ball, right "English" for the left-hand ball.

No. 61.

TO PICK UP A QUARTER.

Place a quarter anywhere on the table. The trick is to lift it off the table with the tip of the cue. For example: Place the tip of the cue on the edge of the quarter nearest to yourself. Press down gently but firmly, drawing the cue toward yourself. The quarter should turn over on the cue and balance itself there, and you can lift it from the table.

No. 62.

TO BALANCE A COIN.

Stand a coin on its edge between two balls on the billiard spot, a steady hand will soon balance it. Then play with another ball from balk at the two other balls, and try and knock down the coin. You will find it stands up as frequently as you knock it down.

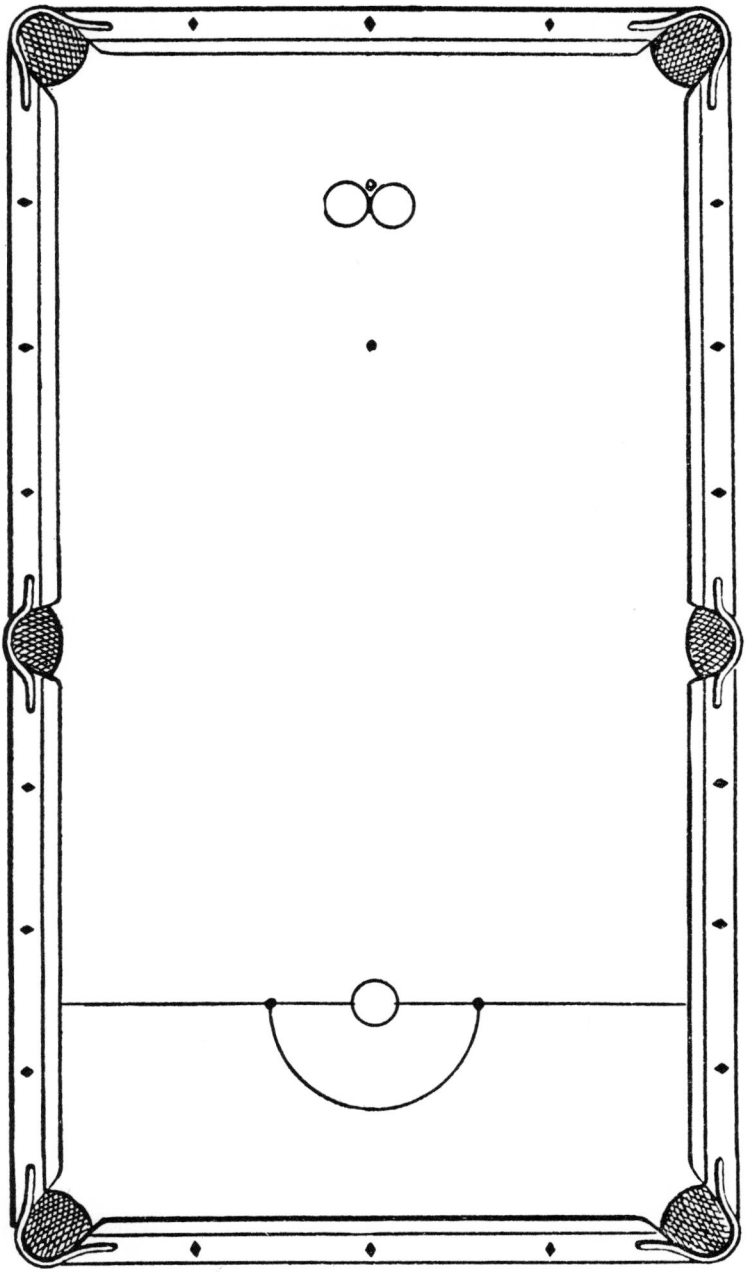

No. 60.

No. 63.

TO POCKET A WINEGLASS.

The following trick comes as a surprise to many, and as a rule long odds are bet against its performance, but in reality the odds are considerably in favor of its being done. Remove the balls from the table before beginning. Get an ordinary sherry glass and roll it gently on its side along the table to see that it has a little bias—that is, when rolling it describes part of a circle, one that rolls straight on is absolutely useless. The trick is, to lay it up against a cushion as in the illustration, and with a push to roll it into and make it disappear in the bottom pocket on the same side. When once you have found the spot to place it, it is almost a certainty. To find the correct spot, place the glass in the jaws of the bottom pocket with the mouth pointing toward the top pocket same side, then place a finger on the stem of the glass and give it a little push off. It should roll round on to the right-hand side cushion. Carefully observe where the base of the glass touches, and you will then have about the spot to place the glass for the return journey. It is well to know your glass to dispense with these preliminaries. Be careful in pushing if off not to let it slide along under the finger; place the pad of the tip of the second finger on the stem, give one push and let go. See illustration for position and the line the glass should go. Try it with several glasses, as some make more extensive curves than others.

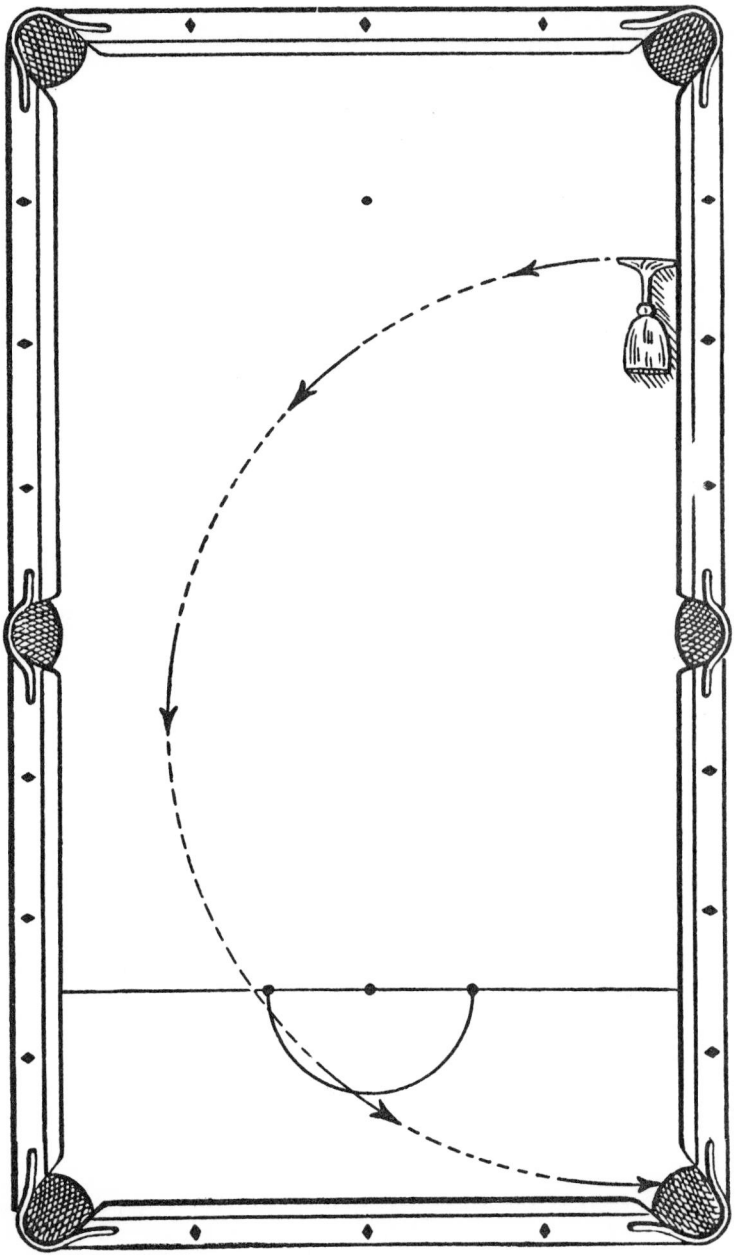

No. 63.

No. 64.

RACE HORSES.

An amusing and speculative game, although it cannot be played with much fun unless there is an amateur bookmaker, who, as a rule, makes a nice little profit. Lay a cue on the table up against an end cushion, and put some pool balls up against it in any order as in illustration. The booky pushes the balls straight down the table with the cue, hard or soft according to the general desire, and removes the cue. That ball wins the race which is nearest to the cushion where they started from when they have all stopped. To facilitate the betting, draw some chalk lines along the cushion and number the spaces between them, one space for each ball running. These numbers refer to the pool balls in the usual order of play: No. 1 white, No. 2 red, No. 3 yellow, etc. Anybody wanting to back his color places the stake on its number. There should always be one ball running for the bookmaker, therefore he should lay odds as follows: However many balls are running he should lay one point less than their number to 1. Eight balls running, 7 to 1, etc. Dead heats of several sometimes happen, when the stakes are divided. When one race is squared up, start again.

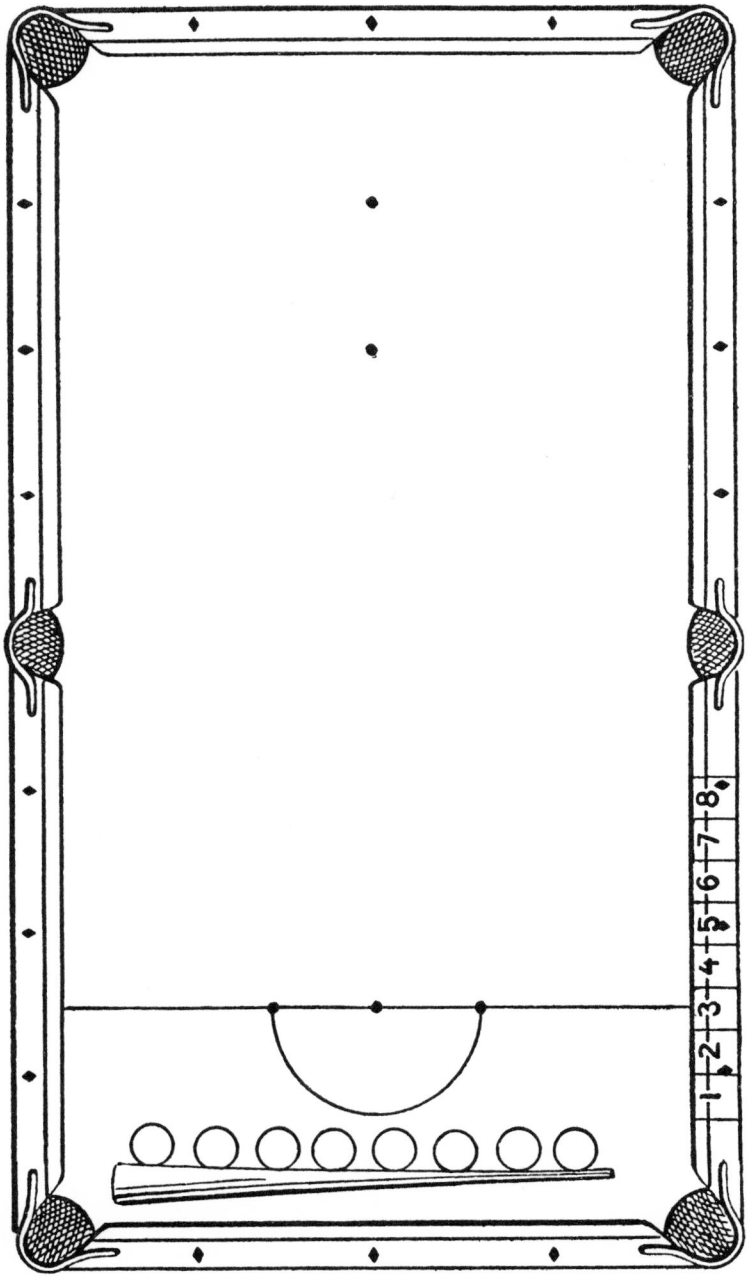

No. 64.

No. 65.

INTERESTING TRICKS IN ELASTICITY.

The clever trick with pool balls shown in Figs. 1 and 2 depends for its success on a truly scientific principle. A number of pool balls are placed in a row against the cushion of the table. The player asks one of the spectators to name a certain number of balls to be pocketed without any apparent disturbance of the others. Suppose the number to be three. Then at the will of the player three balls separate from the others and roll into the pocket. The number is perfectly controllable, and when the hand of the player and one end of the row of balls are covered, the trick appears mysterious. It is hardly less so when the entire experiment is visible. The feat is accomplished by removing from one end of the series as many balls as are to be projected from the opposite end, and rolling them forward against the end of the row remaining. An equal number of balls fly off from the opposite end of the row and roll into the pocket. Three balls driven against one end of the series will cause three to roll off, two will drive off two, one will drive off one, and so on.

The principle of this trick is illustrated in the well-known class-room experiment in which a series of contracting suspended balls of highly elastic material are made to transmit a blow delivered on the first of the series to the last ball of the series, so that the last ball will fly off without any apparent disturbance of the other balls. In this experiment,

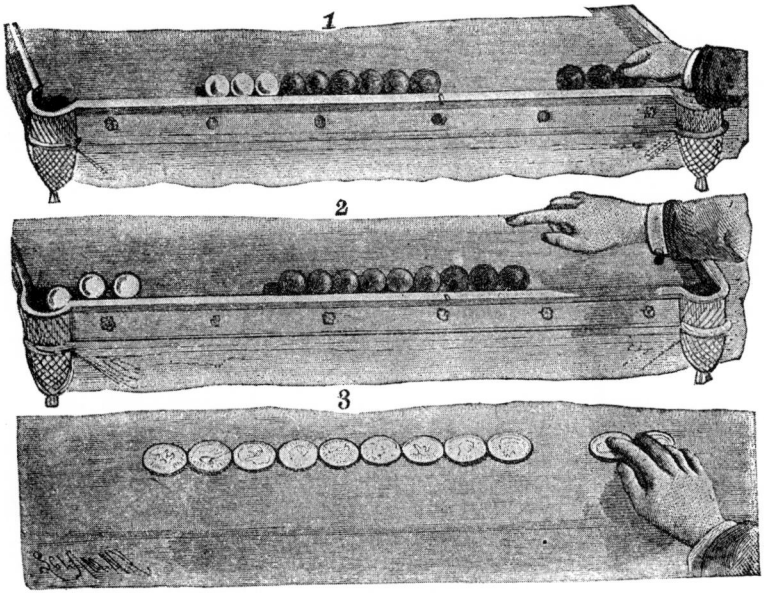

From "Magic." Copyright, 1897, by Munroe & Co.

the first ball of the series is drawn back and allowed to fall against the first one of those remaining in contact. The impact of this ball will slightly flatten the ball with which it comes in contact, and each ball in turn transmits its momentum to the next, and so on through the entire series, the last of the series being thrown out as indicated.

In the case of the experiment with the pool balls, it is found by careful observation that separate blows are given to the series, corresponding in number to the number of balls removed, so that while the separation of the balls at the end of the series is apparently simultaneous, in reality they are separated one at a time.

In Fig. 3 is illustrated a method of repeating the experiment with coins in lieu of balls. Dollars or half-dollars may be used, and the effect is produced by sliding the coins.

No. 66.

TO POCKET THREE BALLS IN THE OPPOSITE MIDDLE POCKET IN TWO SHOTS.

Place the red and the white ball touching each other in the middle of the table, straight between the middle pockets, and place a third ball in balk, as in illustration. The trick is to pocket the three balls in the middle pockets in two shots, the two balls in the centre of the table to go into opposite middle pockets. For example: Play the ball in balk into one of the middle pockets, then hold your cue tightly by the butt with one hand and hit down sharply and truly between the two balls on the table, which should separate and each go into a middle pocket.

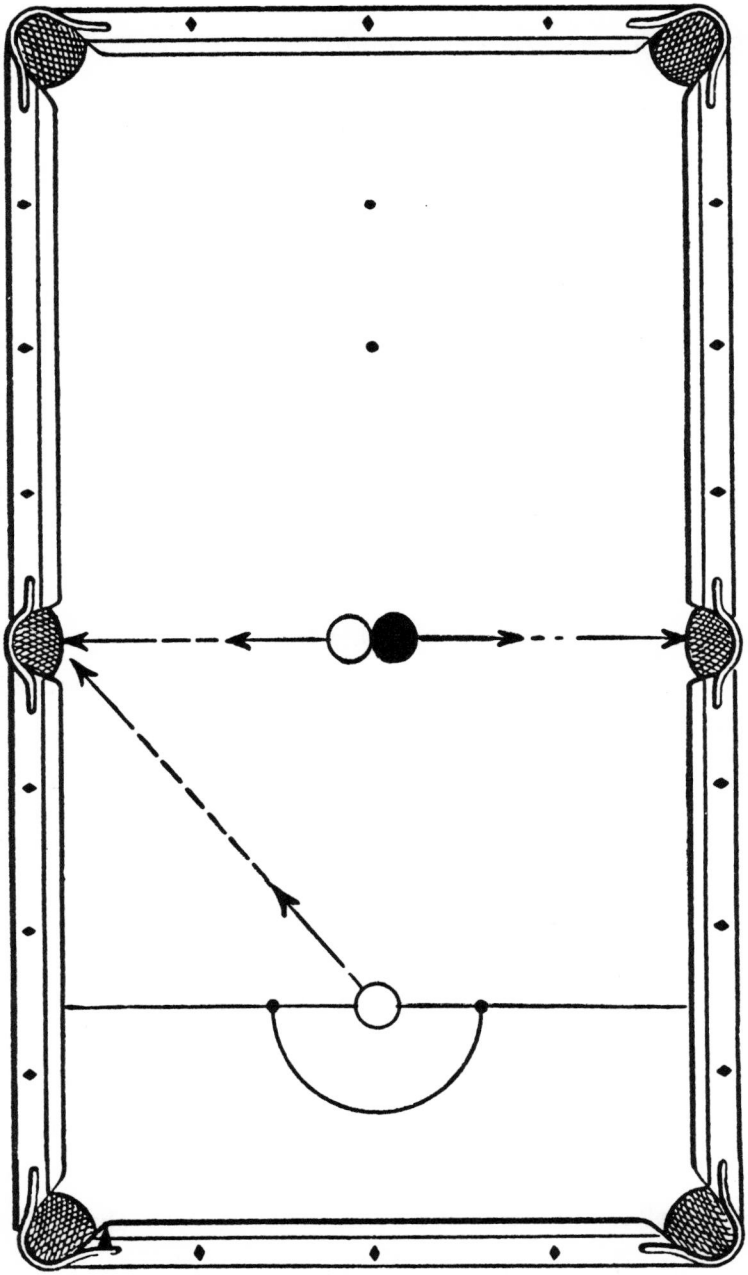

No. 66.

No. 67.

CHANCE ENCOUNTER CAROM.

The following is a pretty shot when it comes off, but is by no means a certainty. Place the red and white, touching each other against a cushion, the red ten inches from the pocket, the white inside it, and place another white four inches behind the white ball touching the red. The shot is to make a carom at the bottom of the table, playing with the ball nearest the pocket. For example: Hit the white about quarter ball right, with sufficient strength for your own ball to go over to the opposite cushion and then cross over to the bottom pocket. The red from the impact will travel straight and slowly down the table, and if you have just gauged the strength the two balls should meet. (See illustration for the idea.)

No. 68.

ONE BALL ON THREE.

Put three balls together and try to balance another ball on top of them. You will find this very difficult to do unless you chalk the top ball on the spots where it will rest on the other balls. To chalk it successfully, rub some chalk into the palm of the hand and rub the top ball on it.

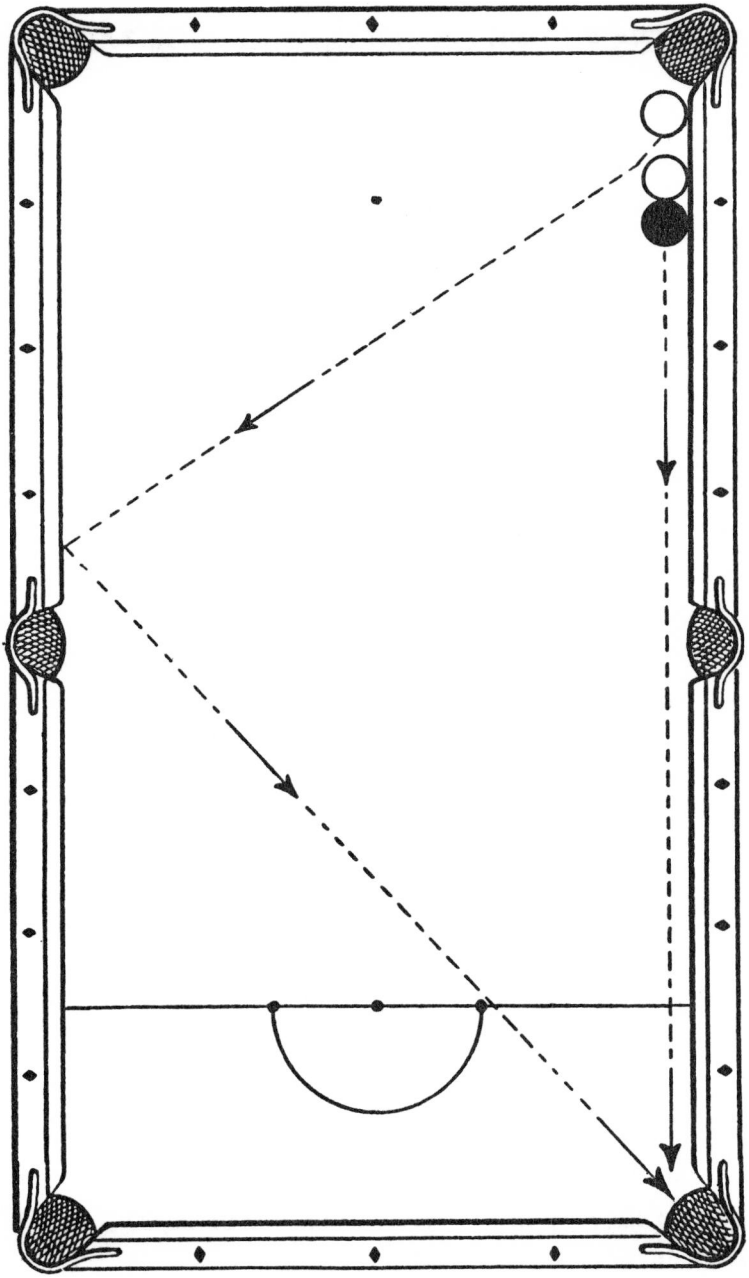

No. 67.

No. 69.

FINE CAROM.

A pretty carom can be made by placing the balls in the positions shown in illustration. Place the red twenty inches from the top pocket, touching the cushion, with a white touching it on the inside (*i.e.*, nearer the middle), and place another white ball in balk ten inches from the right-hand cushion. The shot is to play with the ball from balk and make a carom from the red to the white. For example: Although you can hardly see the red, it is fairly easy to hit it, of course very fine. Put right "English" on your ball, and you should come back on to the white after hitting the top cushion. See dotted lines in illustration.

No. 70.

PICK UP A BALL WITH TWO OTHERS.

Take a ball in each hand, and try and pick up another ball by squeezing it between the balls held in either hand. For example: Press the two balls in the hands, one on each side of the very centre of the third ball, as tightly and truly as you can. If you press accurately and sufficiently hard you can lift it from the table, if not it will slip out and run away on one side or the other.

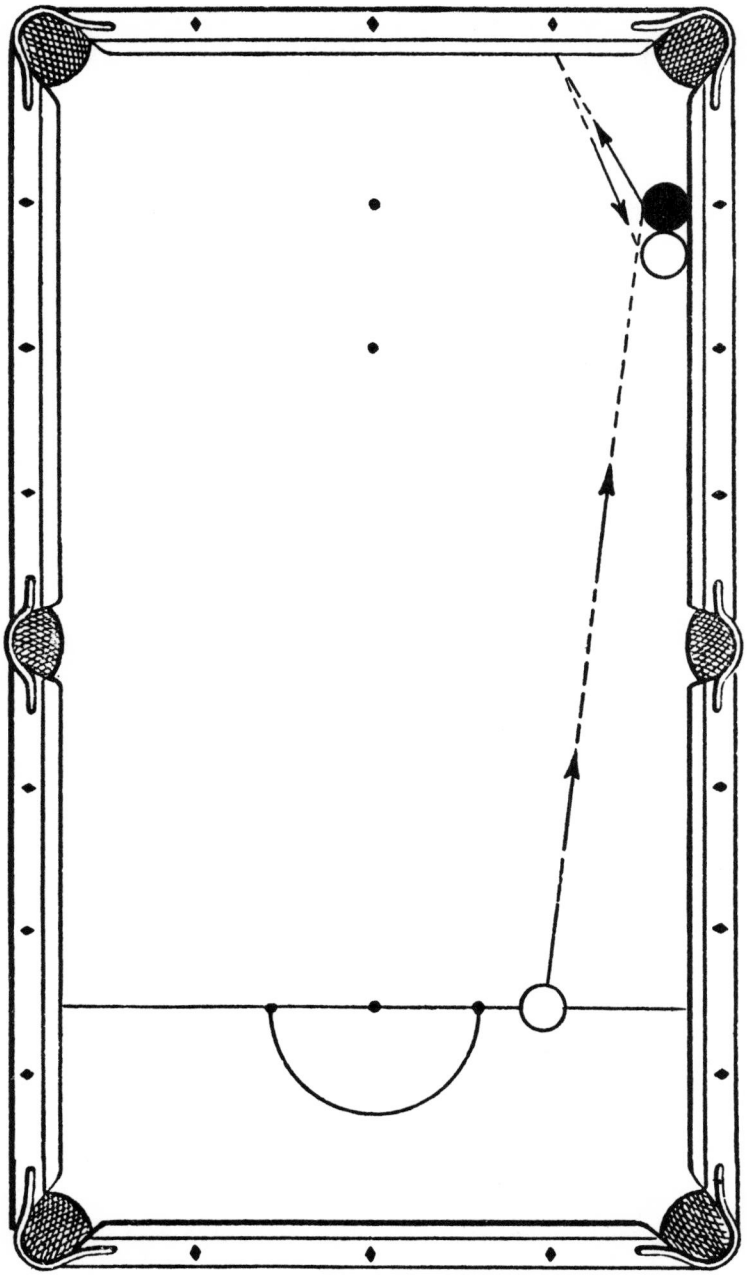

No. 69.

No. 71.

TO POCKET FOUR BALLS IN FOUR SHOTS.

Place five balls on the table as in illustration. The game is to pocket four of them in four shots in the top pockets, only playing with the ball from balk. The player must be satisfied to do it once in a good many attempts. It can be played as a competition, the one who does it in the fewest strokes winning. The idea is, play first at the ball on the right-hand cushion with the ball from balk, play it so that it proceeds slowly along into the right top corner pocket, getting position behind the ball on the spot. Play that one into the left-hand top corner pocket, and try to get down behind the ball on the pyramid spot; send that one into the right-hand top corner pocket, and cross over behind the remaining ball, sending it along the cushion into the left-hand top corner pocket. (See illustration for idea.)

No. 72.

COLLISION SHOT.

Stand close up against the top or bottom cushion, take a ball in each hand, strike them together, not too hard, as close to the middle of the cushion as you can hold them, and let go suddenly. If struck together properly, both balls touching the cushion at the time, they should disappear one in each of the end pockets.

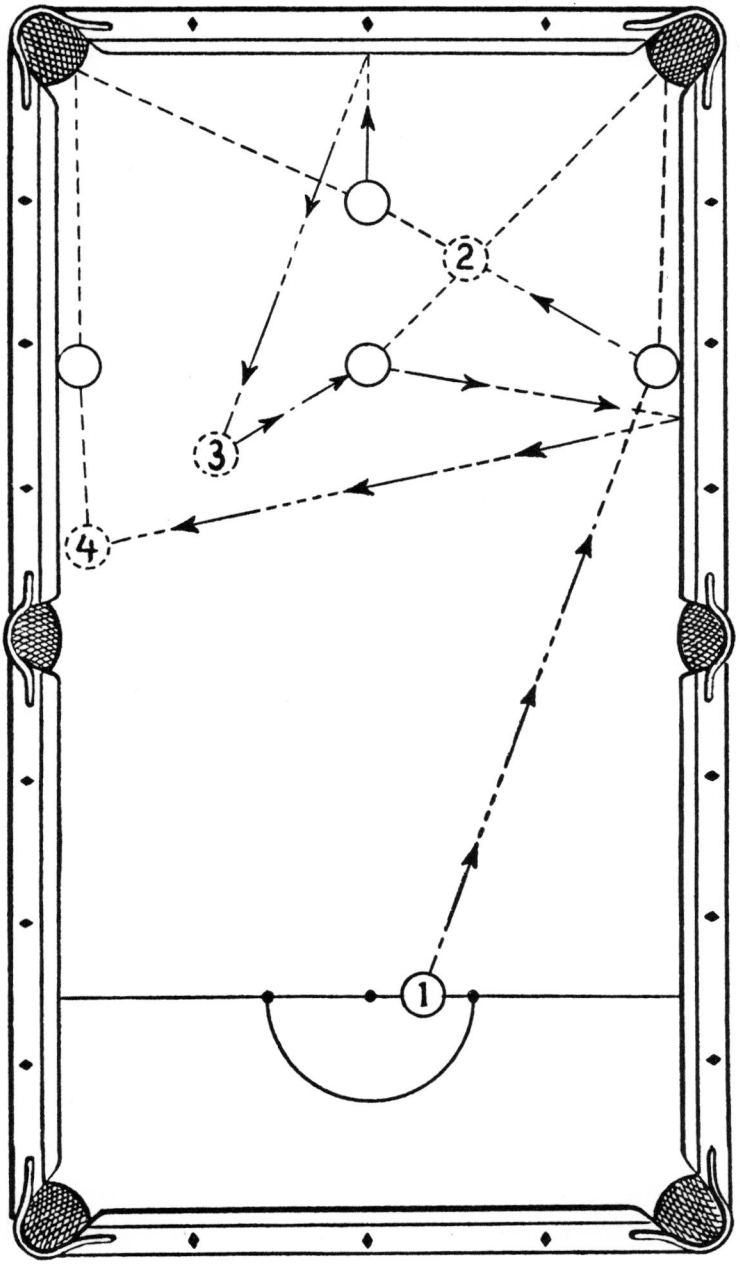

No. 71.

No. 73.

TO JUMP A COIN INTO A GLASS.

To make a coin jump from the cushion into a wineglass.

Place an ordinary wineglass on the woodwork of the table, and place a coin on the cushion at a distance varying from a quarter to three-quarters of an inch from the edge (depending greatly on the hardness or softness of the cushion, as in illustration). Place your ball about a foot from the opposite cushion, in a dead straight line with the coin and middle of the glass. Aim at the coin on the cushion, a moderately hard blow, and it should jump up and fall into the wineglass. One or two trial shots will soon show you how hard to hit your ball and the exact spot to place the coin on the cushion. It can also be done the whole length of the table.

No. 74.

ENDLESS CAROMS.

Put three balls side by side touching. Press the two outer ones *firmly* on the table. Withdraw the middle one, and hit it gently straight through the gap it originally occupied. It will make a double carom on passing between the other two balls, and if the stroke is played sufficiently gently, the two balls when hit will not be displaced from the

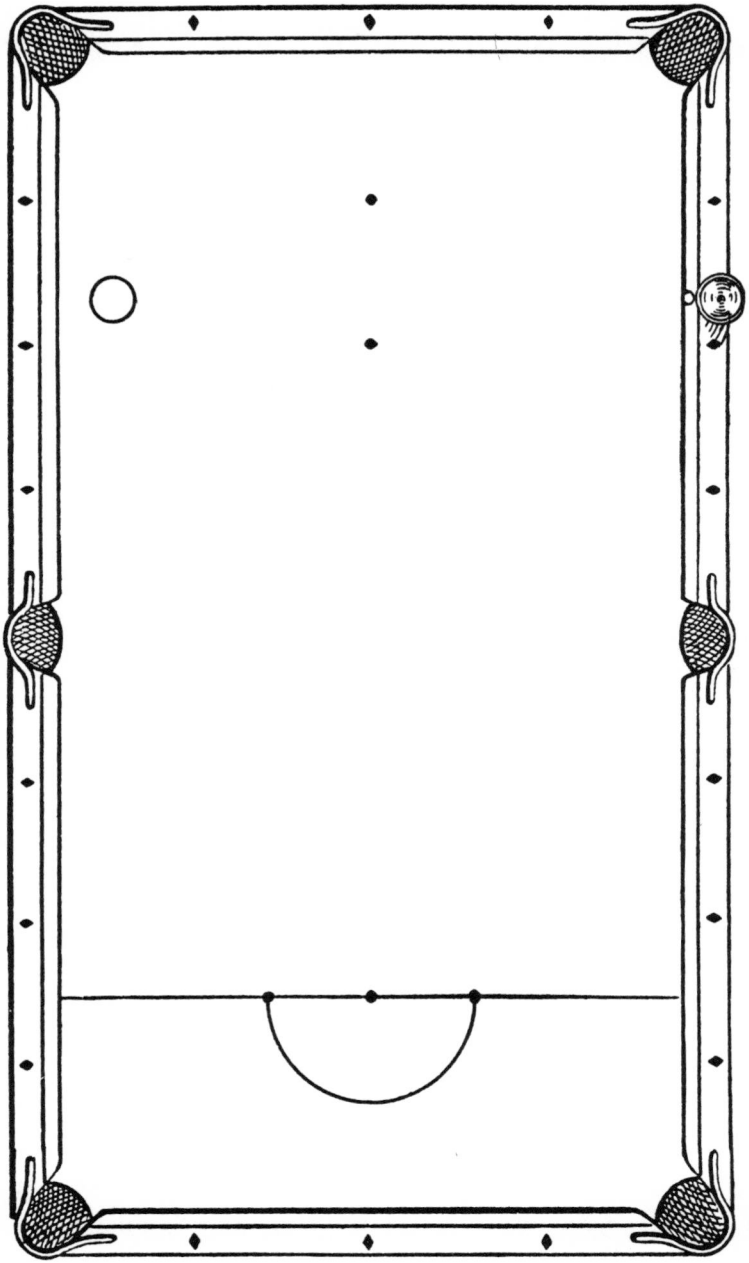

No. 73.

little hollows in which they rest, but will just oscillate, eventually settling down in their original position. A second double carom can now be made by hitting the object ball through the gap in the opposite direction, and so on backward and forward. A fair player with a good eye when once he has judged the correct strength, should be able to make quite fifty double caroms consecutively.

No. 75.

TO POCKET THREE BALLS IN THREE DIFFERENT POCKETS, THREE SHOTS.

Place a ball on the pyramid spot, and another on the middle spot of the D, and a third ball just in front the middle pocket, as in illustration. The trick is: You must stand tight up against the middle pocket where the ball is, and without moving from there you have to pocket all three balls in three shots, one in each pocket of the table the same side as you are standing. For example: Knock the one in nearest to you with the butt of cue. Then lay the cue on the table straight between the middle pockets, the tip toward yourself, hold the tip steady with one hand, with the other catch hold of the cue about half-way down, and sweep it along the cloth at a moderate pace, on to first one and then the other of the balls on the spots, and they should each go into an end pocket.

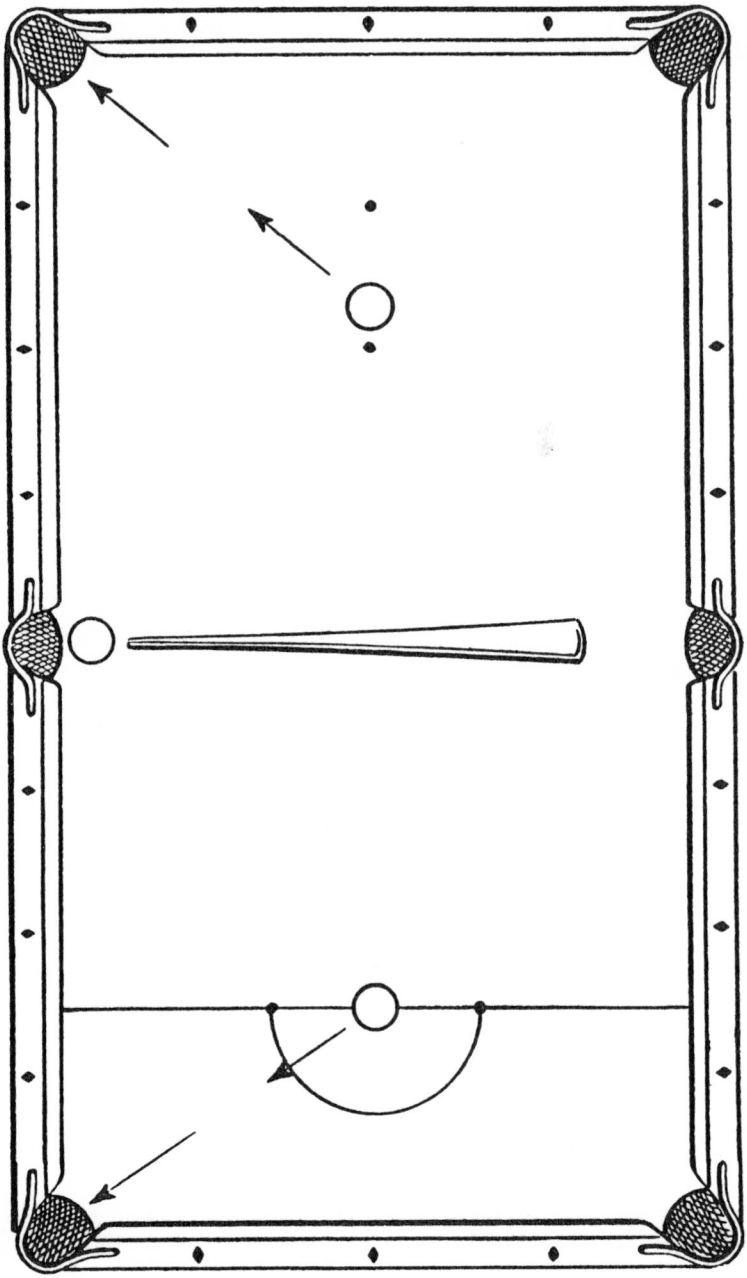

No. 75.

No. 76.

SWITCHBACK CAROM.

An effective carom, and not difficult.

Place the butts of two cues into the left-hand corner bottom pocket, and place the red ball on top of them, as in illustration. Place the spot white against the right-hand cushion in a straight line with the opening of the two cues. The shot is to make a carom from the red to the spot white, playing with the plain white from the D, and hitting the top cushion first. For example: Play almost straight up the table, with a good deal of right side, sufficiently hard that when your ball returns and hits the cues it will jump on to them about one foot from the tips (if hit too hard it will jump over them). Your ball should then run up the cue, hit the red, and start back down again, and if you have put the spot white straight opposite the opening of the two cues, it must hit it.

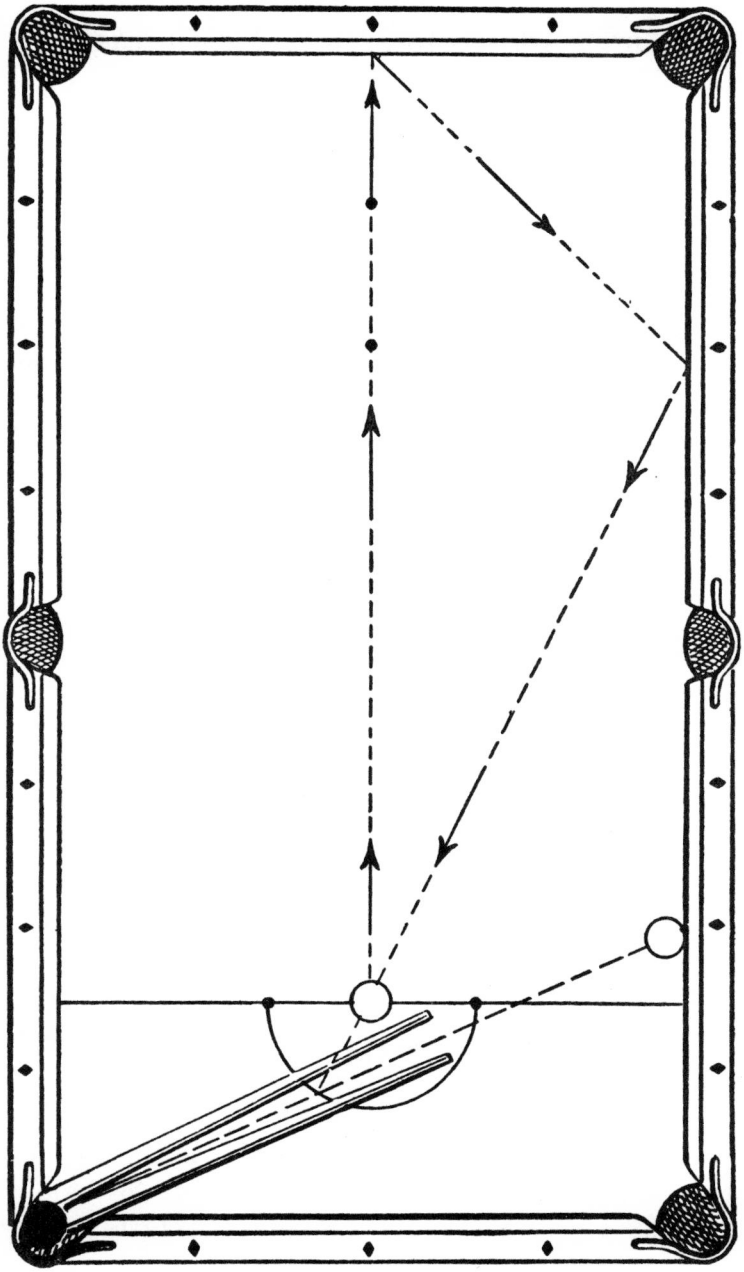

No. 76.

No. 77.

FINE OFF RED BALL.

Place the red on the middle spot of the table and a white on the right-hand spot of the D. The shot is to go in off the red into the left-hand corner top pocket (see dotted lines of illustration). It wants doing, but there is a good margin as you will see if you fail to hit the red. It can be done hard or soft.

No. 78.

WET FINGER TRICK.

This is a trick our grandfathers did. Place your middle finger on a ball and press hard till it slips away, and make it go the length of the table. If you do not wet your finger, you cannot do it.

No. 79.

THE IMPERCEPTIBLE JUMP.

Place three balls absolutely touching in a straight line; draw out the middle one without moving the others, about one foot away from them. The shot is to play with the cue at the ball drawn away from the others, through them without touching either.

For example: Aim straight between the balls, but hit down slightly at your ball, which will cause it to jump quite imperceptibly, sufficient, however, to allow it to pass between the other two without touching. Hit the ball pretty hard.

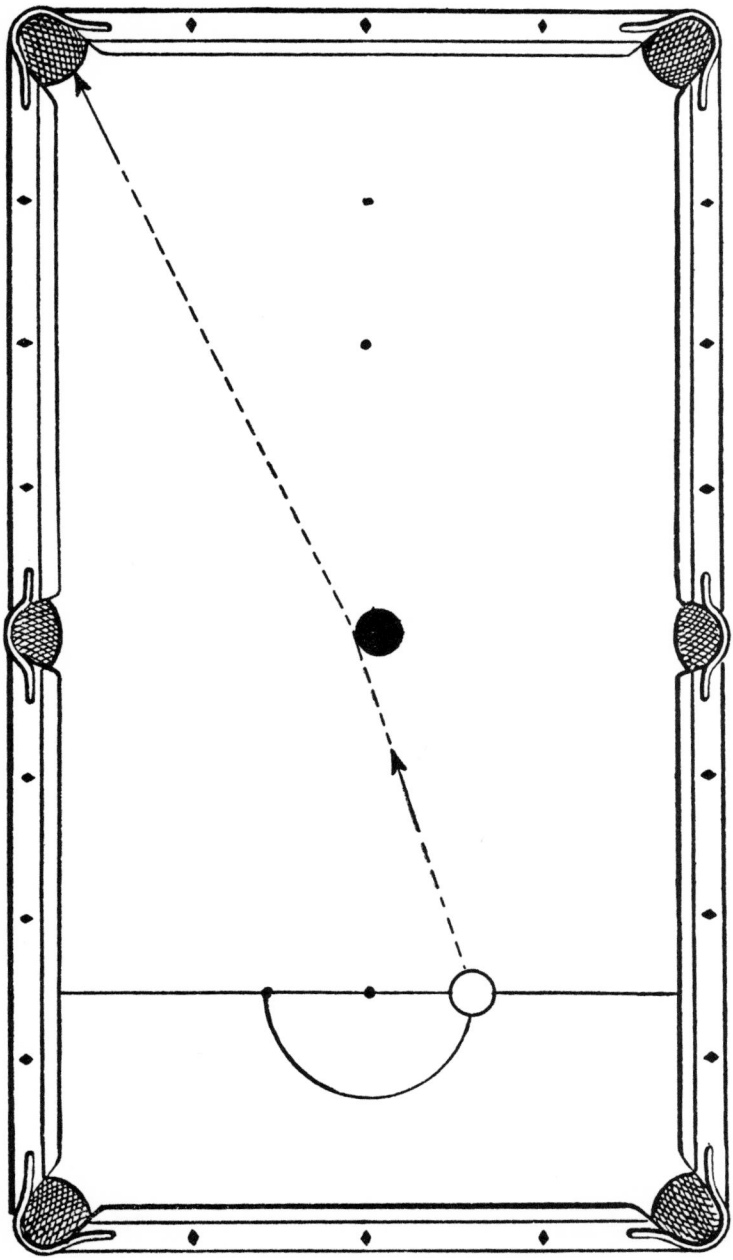

No. 77.

A CATALOG OF SELECTED

DOVER BOOKS

IN ALL FIELDS OF INTEREST

A CATALOG OF SELECTED DOVER BOOKS IN ALL FIELDS OF INTEREST

DRAWINGS OF REMBRANDT, edited by Seymour Slive. Updated Lippmann, Hofstede de Groot edition, with definitive scholarly apparatus. All portraits, biblical sketches, landscapes, nudes. Oriental figures, classical studies, together with selection of work by followers. 550 illustrations. Total of 630pp. 9⅛ × 12¼.
21485-0, 21486-9 Pa., Two-vol. set $29.90

GHOST AND HORROR STORIES OF AMBROSE BIERCE, Ambrose Bierce. 24 tales vividly imagined, strangely prophetic, and decades ahead of their time in technical skill: "The Damned Thing," "An Inhabitant of Carcosa," "The Eyes of the Panther," "Moxon's Master," and 20 more. 199pp. 5⅜ × 8½. 20767-6 Pa. $3.95

ETHICAL WRITINGS OF MAIMONIDES, Maimonides. Most significant ethical works of great medieval sage, newly translated for utmost precision, readability. Laws Concerning Character Traits, Eight Chapters, more. 192pp. 5⅜ × 8½.
24522-5 Pa. $4.50

THE EXPLORATION OF THE COLORADO RIVER AND ITS CANYONS, J. W. Powell. Full text of Powell's 1,000-mile expedition down the fabled Colorado in 1869. Superb account of terrain, geology, vegetation, Indians, famine, mutiny, treacherous rapids, mighty canyons, during exploration of last unknown part of continental U.S. 400pp. 5⅜ × 8½. 20094-9 Pa. $7.95

HISTORY OF PHILOSOPHY, Julián Marías. Clearest one-volume history on the market. Every major philosopher and dozens of others, to Existentialism and later. 505pp. 5⅜ × 8½. 21739-6 Pa. $9.95

ALL ABOUT LIGHTNING, Martin A. Uman. Highly readable non-technical survey of nature and causes of lightning, thunderstorms, ball lightning, St. Elmo's Fire, much more. Illustrated. 192pp. 5⅜ × 8½. 25237-X Pa. $5.95

SAILING ALONE AROUND THE WORLD, Captain Joshua Slocum. First man to sail around the world, alone, in small boat. One of great feats of seamanship told in delightful manner. 67 illustrations. 294pp. 5⅜ × 8½. 20326-3 Pa. $4.95

LETTERS AND NOTES ON THE MANNERS, CUSTOMS AND CONDITIONS OF THE NORTH AMERICAN INDIANS, George Catlin. Classic account of life among Plains Indians: ceremonies, hunt, warfare, etc. 312 plates. 572pp. of text. 6⅛ × 9¼. 22118-0, 22119-9, Pa. Two-vol. set $17.90

ALASKA: The Harriman Expedition, 1899, John Burroughs, John Muir, et al. Informative, engrossing accounts of two-month, 9,000-mile expedition. Native peoples, wildlife, forests, geography, salmon industry, glaciers, more. Profusely illustrated. 240 black-and-white line drawings. 124 black-and-white photographs. 3 maps. Index. 576pp. 5⅜ × 8½. 25109-8 Pa. $11.95

THE BOOK OF BEASTS: Being a Translation from a Latin Bestiary of the Twelfth Century, T. H. White. Wonderful catalog real and fanciful beasts: manticore, griffin, phoenix, amphivius, jaculus, many more. White's witty erudite commentary on scientific, historical aspects. Fascinating glimpse of medieval mind. Illustrated. 296pp. 5⅝ × 8¼. (Available in U.S. only) 24609-4 Pa. $6.95

FRANK LLOYD WRIGHT: ARCHITECTURE AND NATURE With 160 Illustrations, Donald Hoffmann. Profusely illustrated study of influence of nature—especially prairie—on Wright's designs for Fallingwater, Robie House, Guggenheim Museum, other masterpieces. 96pp. 9¼ × 10¾. 25098-9 Pa. $7.95

FRANK LLOYD WRIGHT'S FALLINGWATER, Donald Hoffmann. Wright's famous waterfall house: planning and construction of organic idea. History of site, owners, Wright's personal involvement. Photographs of various stages of building. Preface by Edgar Kaufmann, Jr. 100 illustrations. 112pp. 9¼ × 10.
23671-4 Pa. $8.95

YEARS WITH FRANK LLOYD WRIGHT: Apprentice to Genius, Edgar Tafel. Insightful memoir by a former apprentice presents a revealing portrait of Wright the man, the inspired teacher, the greatest American architect. 372 black-and-white illustrations. Preface. Index. vi + 228pp. 8¼ × 11. 24801-1 Pa. $10.95

THE STORY OF KING ARTHUR AND HIS KNIGHTS, Howard Pyle. Enchanting version of King Arthur fable has delighted generations with imaginative narratives of exciting adventures and unforgettable illustrations by the author. 41 illustrations. xviii + 313pp. 6⅛ × 9¼. 21445-1 Pa. $6.95

THE GODS OF THE EGYPTIANS, E. A. Wallis Budge. Thorough coverage of numerous gods of ancient Egypt by foremost Egyptologist. Information on evolution of cults, rites and gods; the cult of Osiris; the Book of the Dead and its rites; the sacred animals and birds; Heaven and Hell; and more. 956pp. 6⅛ × 9¼.
22055-9, 22056-7 Pa., Two-vol. set $21.90

A THEOLOGICO-POLITICAL TREATISE, Benedict Spinoza. Also contains unfinished *Political Treatise*. Great classic on religious liberty, theory of government on common consent. R. Elwes translation. Total of 421pp. 5⅜ × 8½.
20249-6 Pa. $6.95

INCIDENTS OF TRAVEL IN CENTRAL AMERICA, CHIAPAS, AND YUCATAN, John L. Stephens. Almost single-handed discovery of Maya culture; exploration of ruined cities, monuments, temples; customs of Indians. 115 drawings. 892pp. 5⅜ × 8½. 22404-X, 22405-8 Pa., Two-vol. set $15.90

LOS CAPRICHOS, Francisco Goya. 80 plates of wild, grotesque monsters and caricatures. Prado manuscript included. 183pp. 6⅝ × 9⅜. 22384-1 Pa. $5.95

AUTOBIOGRAPHY: The Story of My Experiments with Truth, Mohandas K. Gandhi. Not hagiography, but Gandhi in his own words. Boyhood, legal studies, purification, the growth of the Satyagraha (nonviolent protest) movement. Critical, inspiring work of the man who freed India. 480pp. 5⅜ × 8½. (Available in U.S. only)
24593-4 Pa. $6.95

ILLUSTRATED DICTIONARY OF HISTORIC ARCHITECTURE, edited by Cyril M. Harris. Extraordinary compendium of clear, concise definitions for over 5,000 important architectural terms complemented by over 2,000 line drawings. Covers full spectrum of architecture from ancient ruins to 20th-century Modernism. Preface. 592pp. 7½ × 9⅜. 24444-X Pa. $15.95

THE NIGHT BEFORE CHRISTMAS, Clement Moore. Full text, and woodcuts from original 1848 book. Also critical, historical material. 19 illustrations. 40pp. 4⅝ × 6. 22797-9 Pa. $2.50

THE LESSON OF JAPANESE ARCHITECTURE: 165 Photographs, Jiro Harada. Memorable gallery of 165 photographs taken in the 1930's of exquisite Japanese homes of the well-to-do and historic buildings. 13 line diagrams. 192pp. 8⅜ × 11¼. 24778-3 Pa. $10.95

THE AUTOBIOGRAPHY OF CHARLES DARWIN AND SELECTED LETTERS, edited by Francis Darwin. The fascinating life of eccentric genius composed of an intimate memoir by Darwin (intended for his children); commentary by his son, Francis; hundreds of fragments from notebooks, journals, papers; and letters to and from Lyell, Hooker, Huxley, Wallace and Henslow. xi + 365pp. 5⅜ × 8. 20479-0 Pa. $6.95

WONDERS OF THE SKY: Observing Rainbows, Comets, Eclipses, the Stars and Other Phenomena, Fred Schaaf. Charming, easy-to-read poetic guide to all manner of celestial events visible to the naked eye. Mock suns, glories, Belt of Venus, more. Illustrated. 299pp. 5¼ × 8¼. 24402-4 Pa. $7.95

BURNHAM'S CELESTIAL HANDBOOK, Robert Burnham, Jr. Thorough guide to the stars beyond our solar system. Exhaustive treatment. Alphabetical by constellation: Andromeda to Cetus in Vol. 1; Chamaeleon to Orion in Vol. 2; and Pavo to Vulpecula in Vol. 3. Hundreds of illustrations. Index in Vol. 3. 2,000pp. 6⅛ × 9¼. 23567-X, 23568-8, 23673-0 Pa., Three-vol. set $41.85

STAR NAMES: Their Lore and Meaning, Richard Hinckley Allen. Fascinating history of names various cultures have given to constellations and literary and folkloristic uses that have been made of stars. Indexes to subjects. Arabic and Greek names. Biblical references. Bibliography. 563pp. 5⅜ × 8½. 21079-0 Pa. $8.95

THIRTY YEARS THAT SHOOK PHYSICS: The Story of Quantum Theory, George Gamow. Lucid, accessible introduction to influential theory of energy and matter. Careful explanations of Dirac's anti-particles, Bohr's model of the atom, much more. 12 plates. Numerous drawings. 240pp. 5⅜ × 8½. 24895-X Pa. $5.95

CHINESE DOMESTIC FURNITURE IN PHOTOGRAPHS AND MEASURED DRAWINGS, Gustav Ecke. A rare volume, now affordably priced for antique collectors, furniture buffs and art historians. Detailed review of styles ranging from early Shang to late Ming. Unabridged republication. 161 black-and-white drawings, photos. Total of 224pp. 8⅜ × 11¼. (Available in U.S. only) 25171-3 Pa. $13.95

VINCENT VAN GOGH: A Biography, Julius Meier-Graefe. Dynamic, penetrating study of artist's life, relationship with brother, Theo, painting techniques, travels, more. Readable, engrossing. 160pp. 5⅜ × 8½. (Available in U.S. only) 25253-1 Pa. $4.95

HOW TO WRITE, Gertrude Stein. Gertrude Stein claimed anyone could understand her unconventional writing—here are clues to help. Fascinating improvisations, language experiments, explanations illuminate Stein's craft and the art of writing. Total of 414pp. 4⅝ × 6⅝. 23144-5 Pa. $6.95

ADVENTURES AT SEA IN THE GREAT AGE OF SAIL: Five Firsthand Narratives, edited by Elliot Snow. Rare true accounts of exploration, whaling, shipwreck, fierce natives, trade, shipboard life, more. 33 illustrations. Introduction. 353pp. 5⅜ × 8½. 25177-2 Pa. $8.95

THE HERBAL OR GENERAL HISTORY OF PLANTS, John Gerard. Classic descriptions of about 2,850 plants—with over 2,700 illustrations—includes Latin and English names, physical descriptions, varieties, time and place of growth, more. 2,706 illustrations. xlv + 1,678pp. 8½ × 12¼. 23147-X Cloth. $75.00

DOROTHY AND THE WIZARD IN OZ, L. Frank Baum. Dorothy and the Wizard visit the center of the Earth, where people are vegetables, glass houses grow and Oz characters reappear. Classic sequel to *Wizard of Oz*. 256pp. 5⅜ × 8. 24714-7 Pa. $5.95

SONGS OF EXPERIENCE: Facsimile Reproduction with 26 Plates in Full Color, William Blake. This facsimile of Blake's original "Illuminated Book" reproduces 26 full-color plates from a rare 1826 edition. Includes "The Tyger," "London," "Holy Thursday," and other immortal poems. 26 color plates. Printed text of poems. 48pp. 5¼ × 7. 24636-1 Pa. $3.50

SONGS OF INNOCENCE, William Blake. The first and most popular of Blake's famous "Illuminated Books," in a facsimile edition reproducing all 31 brightly colored plates. Additional printed text of each poem. 64pp. 5¼ × 7. 22764-2 Pa. $3.50

PRECIOUS STONES, Max Bauer. Classic, thorough study of diamonds, rubies, emeralds, garnets, etc.: physical character, occurrence, properties, use, similar topics. 20 plates, 8 in color. 94 figures. 659pp. 6⅛ × 9¼. 21910-0, 21911-9 Pa., Two-vol. set $15.90

ENCYCLOPEDIA OF VICTORIAN NEEDLEWORK, S. F. A. Caulfeild and Blanche Saward. Full, precise descriptions of stitches, techniques for dozens of needlecrafts—most exhaustive reference of its kind. Over 800 figures. Total of 679pp. 8⅛ × 11. Two volumes. Vol. 1 22800-2 Pa. $11.95
Vol. 2 22801-0 Pa. $11.95

THE MARVELOUS LAND OF OZ, L. Frank Baum. Second Oz book, the Scarecrow and Tin Woodman are back with hero named Tip, Oz magic. 136 illustrations. 287pp. 5⅜ × 8½. 20692-0 Pa. $5.95

WILD FOWL DECOYS, Joel Barber. Basic book on the subject, by foremost authority and collector. Reveals history of decoy making and rigging, place in American culture, different kinds of decoys, how to make them, and how to use them. 140 plates. 156pp. 7⅞ × 10¾. 20011-6 Pa. $8.95

HISTORY OF LACE, Mrs. Bury Palliser. Definitive, profusely illustrated chronicle of lace from earliest times to late 19th century. Laces of Italy, Greece, England, France, Belgium, etc. Landmark of needlework scholarship. 266 illustrations. 672pp. 6⅛ × 9¼. 24742-2 Pa. $14.95

ILLUSTRATED GUIDE TO SHAKER FURNITURE, Robert Meader. All furniture and appurtenances, with much on unknown local styles. 235 photos. 146pp. 9 × 12. 22819-3 Pa. $8.95

WHALE SHIPS AND WHALING: A Pictorial Survey, George Francis Dow. Over 200 vintage engravings, drawings, photographs of barks, brigs, cutters, other vessels. Also harpoons, lances, whaling guns, many other artifacts. Comprehensive text by foremost authority. 207 black-and-white illustrations. 288pp. 6 × 9. 24808-9 Pa. $8.95

THE BERTRAMS, Anthony Trollope. Powerful portrayal of blind self-will and thwarted ambition includes one of Trollope's most heartrending love stories. 497pp. 5⅜ × 8½. 25119-5 Pa. $9.95

ADVENTURES WITH A HAND LENS, Richard Headstrom. Clearly written guide to observing and studying flowers and grasses, fish scales, moth and insect wings, egg cases, buds, feathers, seeds, leaf scars, moss, molds, ferns, common crystals, etc.—all with an ordinary, inexpensive magnifying glass. 209 exact line drawings aid in your discoveries. 220pp. 5⅜ × 8½. 23330-8 Pa. $4.95

RODIN ON ART AND ARTISTS, Auguste Rodin. Great sculptor's candid, wide-ranging comments on meaning of art; great artists; relation of sculpture to poetry, painting, music; philosophy of life, more. 76 superb black-and-white illustrations of Rodin's sculpture, drawings and prints. 119pp. 8⅜ × 11¼. 24487-3 Pa. $7.95

FIFTY CLASSIC FRENCH FILMS, 1912–1982: A Pictorial Record, Anthony Slide. Memorable stills from Grand Illusion, Beauty and the Beast, Hiroshima, Mon Amour, many more. Credits, plot synopses, reviews, etc. 160pp. 8¼ × 11. 25256-6 Pa. $11.95

THE PRINCIPLES OF PSYCHOLOGY, William James. Famous long course complete, unabridged. Stream of thought, time perception, memory, experimental methods; great work decades ahead of its time. 94 figures. 1,391pp. 5⅜ × 8½. 20381-6, 20382-4 Pa., Two-vol. set $23.90

BODIES IN A BOOKSHOP, R. T. Campbell. Challenging mystery of blackmail and murder with ingenious plot and superbly drawn characters. In the best tradition of British suspense fiction. 192pp. 5⅜ × 8½. 24720-1 Pa. $3.95

CALLAS: PORTRAIT OF A PRIMA DONNA, George Jellinek. Renowned commentator on the musical scene chronicles incredible career and life of the most controversial, fascinating, influential operatic personality of our time. 64 black-and-white photographs. 416pp. 5⅜ × 8¼. 25047-4 Pa. $8.95

GEOMETRY, RELATIVITY AND THE FOURTH DIMENSION, Rudolph Rucker. Exposition of fourth dimension, concepts of relativity as Flatland characters continue adventures. Popular, easily followed yet accurate, profound. 141 illustrations. 133pp. 5⅜ × 8½. 23400-2 Pa. $4.95

HOUSEHOLD STORIES BY THE BROTHERS GRIMM, with pictures by Walter Crane. 53 classic stories—Rumpelstiltskin, Rapunzel, Hansel and Gretel, the Fisherman and his Wife, Snow White, Tom Thumb, Sleeping Beauty, Cinderella, and so much more—lavishly illustrated with original 19th century drawings. 114 illustrations. x + 269pp. 5⅜ × 8½. 21080-4 Pa. $4.95

SUNDIALS, Albert Waugh. Far and away the best, most thorough coverage of ideas, mathematics concerned, types, construction, adjusting anywhere. Over 100 illustrations. 230pp. 5⅜ × 8½. 22947-5 Pa. $4.95

PICTURE HISTORY OF THE NORMANDIE: With 190 Illustrations, Frank O. Braynard. Full story of legendary French ocean liner: Art Deco interiors, design innovations, furnishings, celebrities, maiden voyage, tragic fire, much more. Extensive text. 144pp. 8⅜ × 11¾. 25257-4 Pa. $10.95

THE FIRST AMERICAN COOKBOOK: A Facsimile of "American Cookery," 1796, Amelia Simmons. Facsimile of the first American-written cookbook published in the United States contains authentic recipes for colonial favorites—pumpkin pudding, winter squash pudding, spruce beer, Indian slapjacks, and more. Introductory Essay and Glossary of colonial cooking terms. 80pp. 5⅜ × 8½. 24710-4 Pa. $3.50

101 PUZZLES IN THOUGHT AND LOGIC, C. R. Wylie, Jr. Solve murders and robberies, find out which fishermen are liars, how a blind man could possibly identify a color—purely by your own reasoning! 107pp. 5⅜ × 8½. 20367-0 Pa. $2.50

THE BOOK OF WORLD-FAMOUS MUSIC—CLASSICAL, POPULAR AND FOLK, James J. Fuld. Revised and enlarged republication of landmark work in musico-bibliography. Full information about nearly 1,000 songs and compositions including first lines of music and lyrics. New supplement. Index. 800pp. 5⅝ × 8¼. 24857-7 Pa. $15.95

ANTHROPOLOGY AND MODERN LIFE, Franz Boas. Great anthropologist's classic treatise on race and culture. Introduction by Ruth Bunzel. Only inexpensive paperback edition. 255pp. 5⅜ × 8½. 25245-0 Pa. $6.95

THE TALE OF PETER RABBIT, Beatrix Potter. The inimitable Peter's terrifying adventure in Mr. McGregor's garden, with all 27 wonderful, full-color Potter illustrations. 55pp. 4¼ × 5½. (Available in U.S. only) 22827-4 Pa. $1.75

THREE PROPHETIC SCIENCE FICTION NOVELS, H. G. Wells. *When the Sleeper Wakes, A Story of the Days to Come* and *The Time Machine* (full version). 335pp. 5⅜ × 8½. (Available in U.S. only) 20605-X Pa. $6.95

APICIUS COOKERY AND DINING IN IMPERIAL ROME, edited and translated by Joseph Dommers Vehling. Oldest known cookbook in existence offers readers a clear picture of what foods Romans ate, how they prepared them, etc. 49 illustrations. 301pp. 6⅛ × 9¼. 23563-7 Pa. $7.95

SHAKESPEARE LEXICON AND QUOTATION DICTIONARY, Alexander Schmidt. Full definitions, locations, shades of meaning of every word in plays and poems. More than 50,000 exact quotations. 1,485pp. 6½ × 9¼. 22726-X, 22727-8 Pa., Two-vol. set $29.90

THE WORLD'S GREAT SPEECHES, edited by Lewis Copeland and Lawrence W. Lamm. Vast collection of 278 speeches from Greeks to 1970. Powerful and effective models; unique look at history. 842pp. 5⅜ × 8½. 20468-5 Pa. $11.95

THE BLUE FAIRY BOOK, Andrew Lang. The first, most famous collection, with many familiar tales: Little Red Riding Hood, Aladdin and the Wonderful Lamp, Puss in Boots, Sleeping Beauty, Hansel and Gretel, Rumpelstiltskin; 37 in all. 138 illustrations. 390pp. 5⅜ × 8½. 21437-0 Pa. $6.95

THE STORY OF THE CHAMPIONS OF THE ROUND TABLE, Howard Pyle. Sir Launcelot, Sir Tristram and Sir Percival in spirited adventures of love and triumph retold in Pyle's inimitable style. 50 drawings, 31 full-page. xviii + 329pp. 6½ × 9¼. 21883-X Pa. $7.95

AUDUBON AND HIS JOURNALS, Maria Audubon. Unmatched two-volume portrait of the great artist, naturalist and author contains his journals, an excellent biography by his granddaughter, expert annotations by the noted ornithologist, Dr. Elliott Coues, and 37 superb illustrations. Total of 1,200pp. 5⅜ × 8.
Vol. I 25143-8 Pa. $8.95
Vol. II 25144-6 Pa. $8.95

GREAT DINOSAUR HUNTERS AND THEIR DISCOVERIES, Edwin H. Colbert. Fascinating, lavishly illustrated chronicle of dinosaur research, 1820's to 1960. Achievements of Cope, Marsh, Brown, Buckland, Mantell, Huxley, many others. 384pp. 5¼ × 8¼. 24701-5 Pa. $7.95

THE TASTEMAKERS, Russell Lynes. Informal, illustrated social history of American taste 1850's–1950's. First popularized categories Highbrow, Lowbrow, Middlebrow. 129 illustrations. New (1979) afterword. 384pp. 6 × 9.
23993-4 Pa. $8.95

DOUBLE CROSS PURPOSES, Ronald A. Knox. A treasure hunt in the Scottish Highlands, an old map, unidentified corpse, surprise discoveries keep reader guessing in this cleverly intricate tale of financial skullduggery. 2 black-and-white maps. 320pp. 5⅜ × 8½. (Available in U.S. only) 25032-6 Pa. $6.95

AUTHENTIC VICTORIAN DECORATION AND ORNAMENTATION IN FULL COLOR: 46 Plates from "Studies in Design," Christopher Dresser. Superb full-color lithographs reproduced from rare original portfolio of a major Victorian designer. 48pp. 9¼ × 12¼. 25083-0 Pa. $7.95

PRIMITIVE ART, Franz Boas. Remains the best text ever prepared on subject, thoroughly discussing Indian, African, Asian, Australian, and, especially, Northern American primitive art. Over 950 illustrations show ceramics, masks, totem poles, weapons, textiles, paintings, much more. 376pp. 5⅜ × 8. 20025-6 Pa. $7.95

SIDELIGHTS ON RELATIVITY, Albert Einstein. Unabridged republication of two lectures delivered by the great physicist in 1920–21. *Ether and Relativity* and *Geometry and Experience*. Elegant ideas in non-mathematical form, accessible to intelligent layman. vi + 56pp. 5⅜ × 8½. 24511-X Pa. $2.95

THE WIT AND HUMOR OF OSCAR WILDE, edited by Alvin Redman. More than 1,000 ripostes, paradoxes, wisecracks: Work is the curse of the drinking classes, I can resist everything except temptation, etc. 258pp. 5⅜ × 8½. 20602-5 Pa. $4.95

ADVENTURES WITH A MICROSCOPE, Richard Headstrom. 59 adventures with clothing fibers, protozoa, ferns and lichens, roots and leaves, much more. 142 illustrations. 232pp. 5⅜ × 8½. 23471-1 Pa. $3.95

PLANTS OF THE BIBLE, Harold N. Moldenke and Alma L. Moldenke. Standard reference to all 230 plants mentioned in Scriptures. Latin name, biblical reference, uses, modern identity, much more. Unsurpassed encyclopedic resource for scholars, botanists, nature lovers, students of Bible. Bibliography. Indexes. 123 black-and-white illustrations. 384pp. 6 × 9. 25069-5 Pa. $8.95

FAMOUS AMERICAN WOMEN: A Biographical Dictionary from Colonial Times to the Present, Robert McHenry, ed. From Pocahontas to Rosa Parks, 1,035 distinguished American women documented in separate biographical entries. Accurate, up-to-date data, numerous categories, spans 400 years. Indices. 493pp. 6½ × 9¼. 24523-3 Pa. $10.95

THE FABULOUS INTERIORS OF THE GREAT OCEAN LINERS IN HISTORIC PHOTOGRAPHS, William H. Miller, Jr. Some 200 superb photographs capture exquisite interiors of world's great "floating palaces"—1890's to 1980's: *Titanic, Ile de France, Queen Elizabeth, United States, Europa,* more. Approx. 200 black-and-white photographs. Captions. Text. Introduction. 160pp. 8⅜ × 11¾. 24756-2 Pa. $9.95

THE GREAT LUXURY LINERS, 1927–1954: A Photographic Record, William H. Miller, Jr. Nostalgic tribute to heyday of ocean liners. 186 photos of Ile de France, Normandie, Leviathan, Queen Elizabeth, United States, many others. Interior and exterior views. Introduction. Captions. 160pp. 9 × 12. 24056-8 Pa. $10.95

A NATURAL HISTORY OF THE DUCKS, John Charles Phillips. Great landmark of ornithology offers complete detailed coverage of nearly 200 species and subspecies of ducks: gadwall, sheldrake, merganser, pintail, many more. 74 full-color plates, 102 black-and-white. Bibliography. Total of 1,920pp. 8⅜ × 11¼. 25141-1, 25142-X Cloth. Two-vol. set $100.00

THE SEAWEED HANDBOOK: An Illustrated Guide to Seaweeds from North Carolina to Canada, Thomas F. Lee. Concise reference covers 78 species. Scientific and common names, habitat, distribution, more. Finding keys for easy identification. 224pp. 5⅜ × 8½. 25215-9 Pa. $6.95

THE TEN BOOKS OF ARCHITECTURE: The 1755 Leoni Edition, Leon Battista Alberti. Rare classic helped introduce the glories of ancient architecture to the Renaissance. 68 black-and-white plates. 336pp. 8⅜ × 11¼. 25239-6 Pa. $14.95

MISS MACKENZIE, Anthony Trollope. Minor masterpieces by Victorian master unmasks many truths about life in 19th-century England. First inexpensive edition in years. 392pp. 5⅜ × 8½. 25201-9 Pa. $8.95

THE RIME OF THE ANCIENT MARINER, Gustave Doré, Samuel Taylor Coleridge. Dramatic engravings considered by many to be his greatest work. The terrifying space of the open sea, the storms and whirlpools of an unknown ocean, the ice of Antarctica, more—all rendered in a powerful, chilling manner. Full text. 38 plates. 77pp. 9¼ × 12. 22305-1 Pa. $4.95

THE EXPEDITIONS OF ZEBULON MONTGOMERY PIKE, Zebulon Montgomery Pike. Fascinating first-hand accounts (1805–6) of exploration of Mississippi River, Indian wars, capture by Spanish dragoons, much more. 1,088pp. 5⅜ × 8½. 25254-X, 25255-8 Pa. Two-vol. set $25.90

A CONCISE HISTORY OF PHOTOGRAPHY: Third Revised Edition, Helmut Gernsheim. Best one-volume history—camera obscura, photochemistry, daguerreotypes, evolution of cameras, film, more. Also artistic aspects—landscape, portraits, fine art, etc. 281 black-and-white photographs. 26 in color. 176pp. 8⅜ × 11¼. 25128-4 Pa. $13.95

THE DORÉ BIBLE ILLUSTRATIONS, Gustave Doré. 241 detailed plates from the Bible: the Creation scenes, Adam and Eve, Flood, Babylon, battle sequences, life of Jesus, etc. Each plate is accompanied by the verses from the King James version of the Bible. 241pp. 9 × 12. 23004-X Pa. $9.95

HUGGER-MUGGER IN THE LOUVRE, Elliot Paul. Second Homer Evans mystery-comedy. Theft at the Louvre involves sleuth in hilarious, madcap caper. "A knockout."—Books. 336pp. 5⅜ × 8½. 25185-3 Pa. $5.95

FLATLAND, E. A. Abbott. Intriguing and enormously popular science-fiction classic explores the complexities of trying to survive as a two-dimensional being in a three-dimensional world. Amusingly illustrated by the author. 16 illustrations. 103pp. 5⅜ × 8½. 20001-9 Pa. $2.50

THE HISTORY OF THE LEWIS AND CLARK EXPEDITION, Meriwether Lewis and William Clark, edited by Elliott Coues. Classic edition of Lewis and Clark's day-by-day journals that later became the basis for U.S. claims to Oregon and the West. Accurate and invaluable geographical, botanical, biological, meteorological and anthropological material. Total of 1,508pp. 5⅜ × 8½.
21268-8, 21269-6, 21270-X Pa. Three-vol. set $26.85

LANGUAGE, TRUTH AND LOGIC, Alfred J. Ayer. Famous, clear introduction to Vienna, Cambridge schools of Logical Positivism. Role of philosophy, elimination of metaphysics, nature of analysis, etc. 160pp. 5⅜ × 8½. (Available in U.S. and Canada only) 20010-8 Pa. $3.95

MATHEMATICS FOR THE NONMATHEMATICIAN, Morris Kline. Detailed, college-level treatment of mathematics in cultural and historical context, with numerous exercises. For liberal arts students. Preface. Recommended Reading Lists. Tables. Index. Numerous black-and-white figures. xvi + 641pp. 5⅜ × 8½.
24823-2 Pa. $11.95

HANDBOOK OF PICTORIAL SYMBOLS, Rudolph Modley. 3,250 signs and symbols, many systems in full; official or heavy commercial use. Arranged by subject. Most in Pictorial Archive series. 143pp. 8⅛ × 11. 23357-X Pa. $6.95

INCIDENTS OF TRAVEL IN YUCATAN, John L. Stephens. Classic (1843) exploration of jungles of Yucatan, looking for evidences of Maya civilization. Travel adventures, Mexican and Indian culture, etc. Total of 669pp. 5⅜ × 8½.
20926-1, 20927-X Pa., Two-vol. set $11.90

DEGAS: An Intimate Portrait, Ambroise Vollard. Charming, anecdotal memoir by famous art dealer of one of the greatest 19th-century French painters. 14 black-and-white illustrations. Introduction by Harold L. Van Doren. 96pp. 5⅜ × 8½.
25131-4 Pa. $4.95

PERSONAL NARRATIVE OF A PILGRIMAGE TO ALMANDINAH AND MECCAH, Richard Burton. Great travel classic by remarkably colorful personality. Burton, disguised as a Moroccan, visited sacred shrines of Islam, narrowly escaping death. 47 illustrations. 959pp. 5⅜ × 8½. 21217-3, 21218-1 Pa., Two-vol. set $19.90

PHRASE AND WORD ORIGINS, A. H. Holt. Entertaining, reliable, modern study of more than 1,200 colorful words, phrases, origins and histories. Much unexpected information. 254pp. 5⅜ × 8½. 20758-7 Pa. $5.95

THE RED THUMB MARK, R. Austin Freeman. In this first Dr. Thorndyke case, the great scientific detective draws fascinating conclusions from the nature of a single fingerprint. Exciting story, authentic science. 320pp. 5⅜ × 8½. (Available in U.S. only) 25210-8 Pa. $6.95

AN EGYPTIAN HIEROGLYPHIC DICTIONARY, E. A. Wallis Budge. Monumental work containing about 25,000 words or terms that occur in texts ranging from 3000 B.C. to 600 A.D. Each entry consists of a transliteration of the word, the word in hieroglyphs, and the meaning in English. 1,314pp. 6⅝ × 10.
23615-3, 23616-1 Pa., Two-vol. set $31.90

THE COMPLEAT STRATEGYST: Being a Primer on the Theory of Games of Strategy, J. D. Williams. Highly entertaining classic describes, with many illustrated examples, how to select best strategies in conflict situations. Prefaces. Appendices. xvi + 268pp. 5⅜ × 8½. 25101-2 Pa. $5.95

THE ROAD TO OZ, L. Frank Baum. Dorothy meets the Shaggy Man, little Button-Bright and the Rainbow's beautiful daughter in this delightful trip to the magical Land of Oz. 272pp. 5⅜ × 8. 25208-6 Pa. $5.95

POINT AND LINE TO PLANE, Wassily Kandinsky. Seminal exposition of role of point, line, other elements in non-objective painting. Essential to understanding 20th-century art. 127 illustrations. 192pp. 6½ × 9¼. 23808-3 Pa. $5.95

LADY ANNA, Anthony Trollope. Moving chronicle of Countess Lovel's bitter struggle to win for herself and daughter Anna their rightful rank and fortune—perhaps at cost of sanity itself. 384pp. 5⅜ × 8½. 24669-8 Pa. $8.95

EGYPTIAN MAGIC, E. A. Wallis Budge. Sums up all that is known about magic in Ancient Egypt: the role of magic in controlling the gods, powerful amulets that warded off evil spirits, scarabs of immortality, use of wax images, formulas and spells, the secret name, much more. 253pp. 5⅜ × 8½. 22681-6 Pa. $4.50

THE DANCE OF SIVA, Ananda Coomaraswamy. Preeminent authority unfolds the vast metaphysic of India: the revelation of her art, conception of the universe, social organization, etc. 27 reproductions of art masterpieces. 192pp. 5⅜ × 8½.
24817-8 Pa. $5.95

CHRISTMAS CUSTOMS AND TRADITIONS, Clement A. Miles. Origin, evolution, significance of religious, secular practices. Caroling, gifts, yule logs, much more. Full, scholarly yet fascinating; non-sectarian. 400pp. 5⅜ × 8½.
23354-5 Pa. $6.95

THE HUMAN FIGURE IN MOTION, Eadweard Muybridge. More than 4,500 stopped-action photos, in action series, showing undraped men, women, children jumping, lying down, throwing, sitting, wrestling, carrying, etc. 390pp. 7⅞ × 10⅝.
20204-6 Cloth. $21.95

THE MAN WHO WAS THURSDAY, Gilbert Keith Chesterton. Witty, fast-paced novel about a club of anarchists in turn-of-the-century London. Brilliant social, religious, philosophical speculations. 128pp. 5⅜ × 8½. 25121-7 Pa. $3.95

A CEZANNE SKETCHBOOK: Figures, Portraits, Landscapes and Still Lifes, Paul Cezanne. Great artist experiments with tonal effects, light, mass, other qualities in over 100 drawings. A revealing view of developing master painter, precursor of Cubism. 102 black-and-white illustrations. 144pp. 8¾ × 6⅝. 24790-2 Pa. $5.95

AN ENCYCLOPEDIA OF BATTLES: Accounts of Over 1,560 Battles from 1479 B.C. to the Present, David Eggenberger. Presents essential details of every major battle in recorded history, from the first battle of Megiddo in 1479 B.C. to Grenada in 1984. List of Battle Maps. New Appendix covering the years 1967–1984. Index. 99 illustrations. 544pp. 6½ × 9¼. 24913-1 Pa. $14.95

AN ETYMOLOGICAL DICTIONARY OF MODERN ENGLISH, Ernest Weekley. Richest, fullest work, by foremost British lexicographer. Detailed word histories. Inexhaustible. Total of 856pp. 6½ × 9¼.
21873-2, 21874-0 Pa., Two-vol. set $17.00

WEBSTER'S AMERICAN MILITARY BIOGRAPHIES, edited by Robert McHenry. Over 1,000 figures who shaped 3 centuries of American military history. Detailed biographies of Nathan Hale, Douglas MacArthur, Mary Hallaren, others. Chronologies of engagements, more. Introduction. Addenda. 1,033 entries in alphabetical order. xi + 548pp. 6½ × 9¼. (Available in U.S. only)
24758-9 Pa. $13.95

LIFE IN ANCIENT EGYPT, Adolf Erman. Detailed older account, with much not in more recent books: domestic life, religion, magic, medicine, commerce, and whatever else needed for complete picture. Many illustrations. 597pp. 5⅜ × 8½.
22632-8 Pa. $8.95

HISTORIC COSTUME IN PICTURES, Braun & Schneider. Over 1,450 costumed figures shown, covering a wide variety of peoples: kings, emperors, nobles, priests, servants, soldiers, scholars, townsfolk, peasants, merchants, courtiers, cavaliers, and more. 256pp. 8⅜ × 11¼. 23150-X Pa. $9.95

THE NOTEBOOKS OF LEONARDO DA VINCI, edited by J. P. Richter. Extracts from manuscripts reveal great genius; on painting, sculpture, anatomy, sciences, geography, etc. Both Italian and English. 186 ms. pages reproduced, plus 500 additional drawings, including studies for *Last Supper, Sforza* monument, etc. 860pp. 7⅞ × 10¾. (Available in U.S. only) 22572-0, 22573-9 Pa., Two-vol. set $31.90

THE ART NOUVEAU STYLE BOOK OF ALPHONSE MUCHA: All 72 Plates from "Documents Decoratifs" in Original Color, Alphonse Mucha. Rare copyright-free design portfolio by high priest of Art Nouveau. Jewelry, wallpaper, stained glass, furniture, figure studies, plant and animal motifs, etc. Only complete one-volume edition. 80pp. 9⅜ × 12¼. 24044-4 Pa. $9.95

ANIMALS: 1,419 COPYRIGHT-FREE ILLUSTRATIONS OF MAMMALS, BIRDS, FISH, INSECTS, ETC., edited by Jim Harter. Clear wood engravings present, in extremely lifelike poses, over 1,000 species of animals. One of the most extensive pictorial sourcebooks of its kind. Captions. Index. 284pp. 9 × 12. 23766-4 Pa. $9.95

OBELISTS FLY HIGH, C. Daly King. Masterpiece of American detective fiction, long out of print, involves murder on a 1935 transcontinental flight—"a very thrilling story"—NY Times. Unabridged and unaltered republication of the edition published by William Collins Sons & Co. Ltd., London, 1935. 288pp. 5⅜ × 8½. (Available in U.S. only) 25036-9 Pa. $5.95

VICTORIAN AND EDWARDIAN FASHION: A Photographic Survey, Alison Gernsheim. First fashion history completely illustrated by contemporary photographs. Full text plus 235 photos, 1840–1914, in which many celebrities appear. 240pp. 6½ × 9¼. 24205-6 Pa. $6.95

THE ART OF THE FRENCH ILLUSTRATED BOOK, 1700–1914, Gordon N. Ray. Over 630 superb book illustrations by Fragonard, Delacroix, Daumier, Doré, Grandville, Manet, Mucha, Steinlen, Toulouse-Lautrec and many others. Preface. Introduction. 633 halftones. Indices of artists, authors & titles, binders and provenances. Appendices. Bibliography. 608pp. 8⅜ × 11¼. 25086-5 Pa. $24.95

THE WONDERFUL WIZARD OF OZ, L. Frank Baum. Facsimile in full color of America's finest children's classic. 143 illustrations by W. W. Denslow. 267pp. 5⅜ × 8½. 20691-2 Pa. $7.95

FRONTIERS OF MODERN PHYSICS: New Perspectives on Cosmology, Relativity, Black Holes and Extraterrestrial Intelligence, Tony Rothman, et al. For the intelligent layman. Subjects include: cosmological models of the universe; black holes; the neutrino; the search for extraterrestrial intelligence. Introduction. 46 black-and-white illustrations. 192pp. 5⅜ × 8½. 24587-X Pa. $7.95

THE FRIENDLY STARS, Martha Evans Martin & Donald Howard Menzel. Classic text marshalls the stars together in an engaging, non-technical survey, presenting them as sources of beauty in night sky. 23 illustrations. Foreword. 2 star charts. Index. 147pp. 5⅜ × 8½. 21099-5 Pa. $3.95

FADS AND FALLACIES IN THE NAME OF SCIENCE, Martin Gardner. Fair, witty appraisal of cranks, quacks, and quackeries of science and pseudoscience: hollow earth, Velikovsky, orgone energy, Dianetics, flying saucers, Bridey Murphy, food and medical fads, etc. Revised, expanded In the Name of Science. "A very able and even-tempered presentation."—The New Yorker. 363pp. 5⅜ × 8. 20394-8 Pa. $6.95

ANCIENT EGYPT: ITS CULTURE AND HISTORY, J. E Manchip White. From pre-dynastics through Ptolemies: society, history, political structure, religion, daily life, literature, cultural heritage. 48 plates. 217pp. 5⅜ × 8½. 22548-8 Pa. $5.95

SIR HARRY HOTSPUR OF HUMBLETHWAITE, Anthony Trollope. Incisive, unconventional psychological study of a conflict between a wealthy baronet, his idealistic daughter, and their scapegrace cousin. The 1870 novel in its first inexpensive edition in years. 250pp. 5⅜ × 8½. 24953-0 Pa. $5.95

LASERS AND HOLOGRAPHY, Winston E. Kock. Sound introduction to burgeoning field, expanded (1981) for second edition. Wave patterns, coherence, lasers, diffraction, zone plates, properties of holograms, recent advances. 84 illustrations. 160pp. 5⅜ × 8¼. (Except in United Kingdom) 24041-X Pa. $3.95

INTRODUCTION TO ARTIFICIAL INTELLIGENCE: SECOND, ENLARGED EDITION, Philip C. Jackson, Jr. Comprehensive survey of artificial intelligence—the study of how machines (computers) can be made to act intelligently. Includes introductory and advanced material. Extensive notes updating the main text. 132 black-and-white illustrations. 512pp. 5⅜ × 8½. 24864-X Pa. $8.95

HISTORY OF INDIAN AND INDONESIAN ART, Ananda K. Coomaraswamy. Over 400 illustrations illuminate classic study of Indian art from earliest Harappa finds to early 20th century. Provides philosophical, religious and social insights. 304pp. 6⅝ × 9⅜. 25005-9 Pa. $9.95

THE GOLEM, Gustav Meyrink. Most famous supernatural novel in modern European literature, set in Ghetto of Old Prague around 1890. Compelling story of mystical experiences, strange transformations, profound terror. 13 black-and-white illustrations. 224pp. 5⅜ × 8½. (Available in U.S. only) 25025-3 Pa. $6.95

PICTORIAL ENCYCLOPEDIA OF HISTORIC ARCHITECTURAL PLANS, DETAILS AND ELEMENTS: With 1,880 Line Drawings of Arches, Domes, Doorways, Facades, Gables, Windows, etc., John Theodore Haneman. Sourcebook of inspiration for architects, designers, others. Bibliography. Captions. 141pp. 9 × 12. 24605-1 Pa. $7.95

BENCHLEY LOST AND FOUND, Robert Benchley. Finest humor from early 30's, about pet peeves, child psychologists, post office and others. Mostly unavailable elsewhere. 73 illustrations by Peter Arno and others. 183pp. 5⅜ × 8½. 22410-4 Pa. $4.95

ERTÉ GRAPHICS, Erté. Collection of striking color graphics: *Seasons, Alphabet, Numerals, Aces* and *Precious Stones*. 50 plates, including 4 on covers. 48pp. 9⅜ × 12¼. 23580-7 Pa. $7.95

THE JOURNAL OF HENRY D. THOREAU, edited by Bradford Torrey, F. H. Allen. Complete reprinting of 14 volumes, 1837–61, over two million words; the sourcebooks for *Walden*, etc. Definitive. All original sketches, plus 75 photographs. 1,804pp. 8½ × 12¼. 20312-3, 20313-1 Cloth., Two-vol. set $120.00

CASTLES: THEIR CONSTRUCTION AND HISTORY, Sidney Toy. Traces castle development from ancient roots. Nearly 200 photographs and drawings illustrate moats, keeps, baileys, many other features. Caernarvon, Dover Castles, Hadrian's Wall, Tower of London, dozens more. 256pp. 5⅜ × 8¼. 24898-4 Pa. $6.95

CATALOG OF DOVER BOOKS

AMERICAN CLIPPER SHIPS: 1833–1858, Octavius T. Howe & Frederick C. Matthews. Fully-illustrated, encyclopedic review of 352 clipper ships from the period of America's greatest maritime supremacy. Introduction. 109 halftones. 5 black-and-white line illustrations. Index. Total of 928pp. 5⅜ × 8½.
25115-2, 25116-0 Pa., Two-vol. set $17.90

TOWARDS A NEW ARCHITECTURE, Le Corbusier. Pioneering manifesto by great architect, near legendary founder of "International School." Technical and aesthetic theories, views on industry, economics, relation of form to function, "mass-production spirit," much more. Profusely illustrated. Unabridged translation of 13th French edition. Introduction by Frederick Etchells. 320pp. 6⅛ × 9¼. (Available in U.S. only) 25023-7 Pa. $8.95

THE BOOK OF KELLS, edited by Blanche Cirker. Inexpensive collection of 32 full-color, full-page plates from the greatest illuminated manuscript of the Middle Ages, painstakingly reproduced from rare facsimile edition. Publisher's Note. Captions. 32pp. 9⅜ × 12¼. 24345-1 Pa. $4.95

BEST SCIENCE FICTION STORIES OF H. G. WELLS, H. G. Wells. Full novel *The Invisible Man,* plus 17 short stories: "The Crystal Egg," "Aepyornis Island," "The Strange Orchid," etc. 303pp. 5⅜ × 8½. (Available in U.S. only)
21531-8 Pa. $6.95

AMERICAN SAILING SHIPS: Their Plans and History, Charles G. Davis. Photos, construction details of schooners, frigates, clippers, other sailcraft of 18th to early 20th centuries—plus entertaining discourse on design, rigging, nautical lore, much more. 137 black-and-white illustrations. 240pp. 6⅛ × 9¼.
24658-2 Pa. $6.95

ENTERTAINING MATHEMATICAL PUZZLES, Martin Gardner. Selection of author's favorite conundrums involving arithmetic, money, speed, etc., with lively commentary. Complete solutions. 112pp. 5⅜ × 8½. 25211-6 Pa. $2.95

THE WILL TO BELIEVE, HUMAN IMMORTALITY, William James. Two books bound together. Effect of irrational on logical, and arguments for human immortality. 402pp. 5⅜ × 8½. 20291-7 Pa. $7.95

THE HAUNTED MONASTERY and THE CHINESE MAZE MURDERS, Robert Van Gulik. 2 full novels by Van Gulik continue adventures of Judge Dee and his companions. An evil Taoist monastery, seemingly supernatural events; overgrown topiary maze that hides strange crimes. Set in 7th-century China. 27 illustrations. 328pp. 5⅜ × 8½. 23502-5 Pa. $6.95

CELEBRATED CASES OF JUDGE DEE (DEE GOONG AN), translated by Robert Van Gulik. Authentic 18th-century Chinese detective novel; Dee and associates solve three interlocked cases. Led to Van Gulik's own stories with same characters. Extensive introduction. 9 illustrations. 237pp. 5⅜ × 8½.
23337-5 Pa. $4.95

Prices subject to change without notice.

Available at your book dealer or write for free catalog to Dept. GI, Dover Publications, Inc., 31 East 2nd St., Mineola, N.Y. 11501. Dover publishes more than 175 books each year on science, elementary and advanced mathematics, biology, music, art, literary history, social sciences and other areas.